NCERT SOLUTIONS

Economics

CLASS
12

NCERT SOLUTIONS

Economics

CLASS **12**

by
CK Yadav

arihant

Arihant Prakashan (School Division Series)

✳ arihant

Arihant Prakashan (School Division Series)

All Rights Reserved

ꙮ **Administrative & Production Offices**

Regd. Office

'Ramchhaya' 4577/15, Agarwal Road, Darya Ganj, New Delhi -110002
Tele: 011- 47630600, 43518550

ꙮ **Head Office**

Kalindi, TP Nagar, Meerut (UP) - 250002
Tel: 0121-7156203, 7156204

ꙮ **Sales & Support Offices**

Agra, Ahmedabad, Bengaluru, Bareilly, Chennai, Delhi, Guwahati, Hyderabad, Jaipur, Jhansi, Kolkata, Lucknow, Nagpur & Pune.

ꙮ **ISBN** 978-93-27198-22-5

ꙮ

PO No : TXT-XX-XXXXXXX-X-XX

Published by Arihant Publications (India) Ltd.

For further information about the books published by Arihant, log on to www.arihantbooks.com or e-mail at info@arihantbooks.com

Follow us on   

Preface

Feeling the immense importance and value of NCERT books, we are presenting this book, having the **NCERT Exercises Solutions.** For the overall benefit of the students we have made this book unique in such a way that it presents not only solutions but also detailed explanations. Through these detailed and thorough explanations, students can learn the concepts which will enhance their thinking and learning abilities.

Explanatory Solutions have been provided to all the questions given in each chapter of NCERT book. We have given all the points that tell how to approach to solve a problem. Here we have tried to cover all those loopholes which may lead to confusion. All formulae and hints are discussed in full detail.

Apart from all those who helped in the compilation of this book a special note of thanks to Mr Saurabh Gupta. With the hope that this book will be of great help to the students, I wish great success to my readers.

CK Yadav

Contents

Introductory Microeconomics

1

Introduction

Points to Remember

1. **Economy** Economy refers to the nature and level of economic activities in an area. It shows how the people of the concerned area earn their living.

2. **Types of Economy**
   (i) Market economies are those economies, in which economic activities are left to the free play of the market forces.
   (ii) Centrally planned economies are those economies where the course of economic activities is dictated or decided by some central authority or by the government.
   (iii) Mixed economies share the characteristics of both market and centrally planned economies.

3. **Central Problems of Economy at the Micro Level**
   (i) What to produce?
   (ii) How to produce? or Choice of technique of production.
   (iii) For whom to produce? or Resources of allocation.

4. **Economics** Economics is defined as the allocation of scarce resources in such a manner that our economic welfare is maximised.

5. **Branches of Economics**
   (i) **Micro Economics** It studies the economic issues of an individual unit like an individual consumer, an individual producer etc.
   (ii) **Macro Economics** It studies the economic issues at the level of an economy as a whole live total employment of resources, total national product etc.

6. **PPC** (Production Possibility Curve) It shows different combinations of two goods, which can be produced with given resources and technology.

7. **Opportunity Cost** It is the value of a factor in its next best alternative use.

8. **Marginal Opportunity Cost** The rate at which output in use-1 is lost for every additional unit of output in use-2 $\left(\dfrac{\Delta Q_1}{\Delta Q_2}\right)$ implies marginal opportunity cost.

QR Code Questions

Question 1.

Scarcity is a situation when demand for good is

(a) Less than supply   (b) Equal to supply
(c) More than supply   (d) None of these

Answer (c) More than supply

Question 2. The market form in which there are a few big firms is called ....

(a) Oligopoly   (b) Duopoly
(c) Perfect competition   (d) Monopoly

Answer (a) Oligopoly

This concept is explained in Chapter-6 (Part-A) of NCERT Book.

Question 3. Problem of resources allocation deals with

    (a) From whom to produce

    (b) What to produce

    (c) How to produce

    (d) All of the above

Answer All options given are incorrect. Correct answer is 'For whom to produce'.

Question 4. What is the shape of MR curve in perfect competition market?

    (a) Downward sloping from left to right

    (b) Horizontal line parallel to X axis

    (c) Vertical line parallel to Y axis

    (d) Upward sloping from left to right

Answer (b) Horizontal line parallel to X axis

This concept is explained in Chapter-4 (Part-A) of NCERT Book.

Question 5. Which of the following is the feature of monopolistic competition?

    (a) Differentiated Product

    (b) Two Sellers

    (c) Single Seller

    (d) AR curve of the firm is constant

Answer (a) Differentiated Product

This concept is explained in Chapter-6 (Part-A) of NCERT Book.

Exercises

Question 1. Discuss the central problems of an economy.

Answer We know that resources are limited in relation to the unlimited wants, it is important to economise their use and utilise them in the most efficient manner.

It leads to following central problems, that are faced by every economy.

    (i) **What to Produce?**

        There is limited resources and thus producers can not produce all the goods, in an economy. So, every economy has this problem that what to produce and in what quantities. It has two dimensions

        (a) Kinds of goods to be produced

        (b) Quantity of goods to be produced.

(ii) **How to Produce?**

This problem refers to the selection of technique to be used for production of goods and services.

There are various techniques available to produce goods

(a) Labour Intensive Techniques   (b) Capital Intensive Techniques

Thus, it is difficult to allocate the resources efficiently and effectively.

(iii) **For Whom to Produce?**

Due to lack of resources in every economy, can not satisfy all the wants of its people. So, there is problem to select the category of people who consume the goods. Whether to produce goods for rich section or poor section of society or more for rich and less for poor section.

Thus, every economy faces the problem of allocating the scarce resource to the production of different possible goods and services and distribution of these among the individuals with in the economy. The allocation of scarce resources and the distribution of the final goods and services are the central problem of any economy.

Question 2. What do you mean by the production possibilities of an economy?

Answer We have scarce resources and there is a problem exist what to produce and in what quantity. Thus, we are taking the help from the production possibility curve.

It tells us how we can combine two goods and they can be produced with the given resources on the assumptions that (a) resources are fully and efficiently utilised and (b) technique of production remains constant or we can say production possibility implies the possible situation to produce two goods with given resources and technology.

Question 3. What is a production possibility frontier?

Answer It refers to a graphical representation of all the possible combinations of two products that can be produced with the given resources and technology.

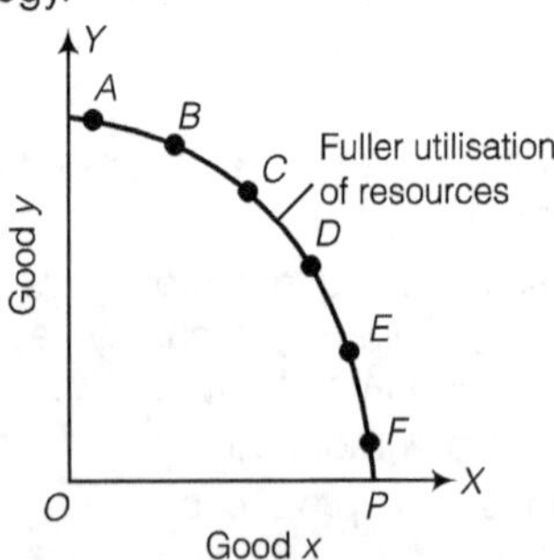

Question 4. Discuss the subject matter of economics.

Answer Traditionally, the subject matter of economics has been studied under two branches *i.e.*,

(i) **Micro Economics** It is that branch of economics, which studies the problems of an individual unit of an economy. Its main tools are demand and supply. *e.g.*, Individual income, individual expenditure.

(ii) **Macro Economics** It is that branch of economics, which studies the economic problems at the level of an economy as a whole. It is concerned with determination of aggregate output and general price level in the economy as a whole. Its main tools are aggregate demand and aggregate supply.

Question 5. Distinguish between a centrally planned economy and a market economy.

Answer Difference between centrally planned economy and market economy

S.N.	Centrally Planned Economy	Market Economy
(i)	It owned, controlled and operated by the government.	It owned, controlled and operated by the private sector.
(ii)	All the means of production are owned by the government in case of centrally planned economy.	All resources of production (land, labour, capital and enterprise) are private property.
(iii)	Government plays the complete role.	Government does not play any role.
(iv)	The central planning authority decides what, how and for whom to produce.	The decisions of what, how and for whom to produce through price mechanism.

Question 6. What do you understand by positive economic analysis?

Answer Positive economic analysis is confined to cause and effect relationship. In other words, it states "what is." It relates to what the facts are, were or will be about various economic phenomena in the economics. *e.g.*, it deals with the analysis of questions like what are the causes of unemployment.

Question 7. What do you understand by normative economic analysis?

Answer Normative economic analysis is concerned with what 'ought to be'. It examines the real economic events from moral and ethical angles and judge whether certain economic events are desirable or undesirables.

e.g., it deals with the analysis of questions like what should be the prices of foodgrains.

Question 8. Distinguish between microeconomics and macroeconomics.

Answer Difference between microeconomics and macroeconomics

Basis	Microeconomics	Macroeconomics
Meaning	It is that part of economics, which studies the economic problems of individual unit.	It is that part of economics, which studies the economic problems of an aggregate level.
Objective	Its aim is determine the commodity price or factors of production for an individual firm.	Its aim is to determine national income, employment and growth of nation in the economy as a whole.
Tools	Its main tools are demand and supply.	Its main tools are aggregate demand and aggregate supply.
Level of Aggregation	It involves limited degree of aggregation.	It involves the highest level of aggregation.
Theory	Related theories are (a) Theory of price (b) Theory of consumer behaviour	Related theories are (a) Theory of multiprice (b) Theory related to gap in economy

2

Theory of Consumer Behaviour

Points to Remember

1. **Utility** Utility is the want satisfying power of the commodity.
2. **Marginal Utility** The marginal utility of a commodity is the change in total utility which results from a unit increase in consumption.

$$MU = TU_n - TU_{n-1} \ \text{ or } \ \frac{\Delta \text{ in TU}}{\Delta \text{ in unit of commodity}}$$

Here, $\quad$ MU = Marginal utility

$\qquad$ TU_n = Total utility of n units of commodity

$\qquad$ TU_{n-1} = Total utility of $n-1$ units of commodity

3. **Total Utility** Total utility is the sum of marginal Utilities obtained from the consumption of different units of a commodity.

$$TU = \Sigma MU$$

Here, $\quad$ TU = Total utility

$\qquad$ ΣMU = Sum of total of marginal utilities

4. **Budget Set** It refers to attainable combinations of a set of two goods, given prices of goods and income of the consumer.
5. **Budget Line** It is a line showing different possible combinations of Good-1 and Good-2, which a consumer can buy, given his budget and the prices of Good-1 and Good-2.

6. **Monotonic Preferences** A consumer preferences are monotonic if and only if between any two bundles. The consumer prefers the bundles, which has more of at least one of the goods and no less of the other good as compared to the other bundle.

7. **Indifference Curve** A curve which is a diagrammatic presentation of an indifference set. It shows different combinations of two commodities between which a consumer is indifferent. Each combination offers him the same level of satisfaction.

8. **Marginal Rate of Substitution** It refers to the rate which the consumer is willing to substitute Good-x for Good-y or it refers to the number of units of Good-y which the consumer is willing to sacrifice for an additional unit of Good-x, it is expressed as $\dfrac{\Delta y}{\Delta x}$.

9. **Diminishing Rate of Substitution** The law states that as good-1 is substitution for good-2, the marginal rate of substitution of good-1 for good-2 goes on diminishing.

10. **Indifference Map** The collection of indifference curve is called indifference map.

11. **Properties of Indifference Curve**
    (i) Indifference curves are negatively sloped.
    (ii) Indifference curves are convex to the point of origin.
    (iii) Indifference curves never touch or intersect each other.
    (iv) Indifference curve touches neither X-axis nor Y-axis.

12. **Conditions for Consumer's optimum**
    (i) Budget line should be tangent to the IC.
    (ii) Slope of IC = Slope to the budget line
         (MRS = Price ratio)

13. **Demand** Demand refers to the desire to buy a commodity backed by willingness and ability to purchase that commodity at a given point of time.

    According to **Prof RG Lipsey**, "The amount of a commodity that households wish to purchase is called the quantity demanded of that commodity".

14. **Demand Function**
    $$q_x = F(P_x)$$
    Here, q_x = quantity of x commodity
            P_x = Price of x commodity

15. **Demand Schedule** Tabular presentation of relationship between price and demand of a commodity is called Demand schedule.

16. **Demand Curve** Graphical presentation of relationship between price and demand of a commodity is called Demand curve.

17. **Linear Demand**

$$d = a - bp$$

Here, d = Quantity demanded

a = Vertical intercept

b = Slope of the demand curve

p = Price of the commodity

18. **Law of Demand** The law states that other things remaining the same, the demand for a commodity expands with fall in its price and contracts with a rise in its price.

19. **Exceptions to the Law of Demand**
    (i) Expectations of further changes in price
    (ii) Prestige goods
    (iii) Giffen goods   (iv) Necessities

20. **Determinants of Demand**
    (i)   Price of the commodity
    (ii) Income of the consumer
    (iii) Price of related goods
    (iv) Taste and preference

21. **Normal Goods** It is a good whose demand increases with rise in income and decreases with fall in income of the consumer. *e.g.*, full-cream milk, wheat.

22. **Inferior Goods** It is a good whose demand decreases with rise in income and increases with fall in income of the consumer. *e.g.*, bajra, toned milk.

23. **Giffen Goods** Giffen goods are those inferior goods in case of which there is a positive relationship between price and quantity demanded and inverse relationship between income and quantity demanded.

24. **Cross Price Effect** It refers to change in demand for one commodity owing to change in price of other commodity.

25. **Substitute Goods** These are those goods which can be interchanged for use. If price of the substitute goods increase, the demand for the concerned goods increase and *vice-versa* *e.g.*, tea and coffee.

26. **Complementary Goods** These are those goods which are used simultaneously. If price of one good increases, demand for its complementaries will decrease and *vice-versa*. *e.g.*, pen and ink.

27. **Price Elasticity of Demand** It is the degree of responsiveness of quantity demanded of a commodity to the change in its price.

28. **Methods of Measuring Elasticity of Demand**

    (i) **Percentage Method**

$$e_d = \frac{\% \text{ change in quantity demanded}}{\% \text{ change in price}}$$

    or $\quad \dfrac{\Delta Q}{\Delta P} \times \dfrac{P}{Q}$

    Here, P = Actual price

    $\quad\quad\ Q$ = Actual quantity

    $\quad\quad\ \Delta P$ = Change in price

    $\quad\quad\ \Delta Q$ = Change in quantity

    (ii) **Total Expenditure Method**

    $\quad$ TE $= P \times Q$

    $\quad\ P$ = Price, Q = quantity

    $\quad$ TE = Total expenditure

    (iii) **Geometric or Print Method**

$$e_d = \frac{\text{Lower Segment of demand curve}}{\text{Upper segment of demand curve}}$$

29. **Degrees of Price Elasticity of Demand**

    (i) Perfectly Elastic Demand ($e_d = \infty$)

    (ii) More than unit elastic or elastic demand ($e_d > 1$)

    (iii) Less than unit elastic or inelastic demand ($e_d < 1$)

    (iv) Unit elastic demand ($e_d = 1$)

    (v) Perfectly inelastic demand ($e_d = 0$)

30. **Factors Influencing the Elasticity of Demand**

    (i) Substitute goods

    (ii) Postponement of consumption

    (iii) Proportion of expenditure

    (iv) Nature of the commodity

    (v) Uses of the commodity

    (vi) The time period

    (vii) Income

    (viii) Habbits

QR Code Questions

Question 1. Comment on the nature of goods, if the demand of one good increases due to decrease in the price of another goods.

    (a) Inferior Goods   (b) Complementary Goods

    (c) Substitute Goods   (d) Giffen Goods

Answer (c) Substitute Goods

Question 2. Budget line can not shift right

    (a) When price of both goods increases

    (b) When price of both goods falls

    (c) When the level of income increases

    (d) When price of one good decreases

Answer (a) When price of both goods increases

Question 3. .... is the set of all possible combination of two goods which a consumer can afford, at his given income.

    (a) Marginal rate of substitution

    (b) Indifference curve

    (c) Budget line

    (d) Diminishing marginal rate of substitution

Answer (c) Budget line

Question 4. There is an inverse relation between price and demand for

    (a) Monopoly only

    (b) Both monopoly and monopolistic competition

    (c) Monopolistic competition

    (d) Perfect competition only

Answer (b) Both monopoly and monopolistic competition

    This concept is explained in Chapter-6 (Part-A) of NCERT Book.

Question 5. When the income of consumer falls, the demand curve of an inferior good

    (a) Shift to the left

    (b) Shift to the right

    (c) There is downward movement along the demand curve

    (d) There is upward movement along the demand curve

Answer (b) Shift to the right

Question 6. If there is a rise in the price of coffee consumer may buy tea instead of coffee which effect is this?

    (a) Income Effect

    (b) Substitution Effect

    (c) Price Effect

Answer (b) Substitution Effect

Question 7. When the quantity demanded decreases in response to an increase in consumer income, the good is known as

    (a) Inferior Goods   (b) Normal Goods

    (c) Giffen Goods

    (d) None of the above

Answer (a) Inferior Goods

Question 8. According to Indifference Curve approach, at the point of equilibrium

    (a) Slope of Indifference curve = Slope of Price line

    (b) Slope of Indifference Curve < Slope of Price Line

    (c) Slope of Indifference Curve > Slope of Price Line

    (d) Slope of Indifference curve is not equal to Slope of Price Line

Answer (a) Slope of Indifference curve = Slope of Price line

Question 9. In case of $MUx/Px > MUy/Py$

    (a) Consumer will shift some expenditure from Y to X

    (b) Consumer will shift some expenditure from X to Y

    (c) Consumer will spend less on both X and Y

    (d) Consumer will spend more on both X and Y

Answer (a) Consumer will shift some expenditure from Y to X

Question 10. What does elasticity measure?

    (a) The slope of the demand curve

    (b) Percentage change in one variable in response to one percent change in another variable.

    (c) The percentage change in demand for the good divided by the percentage change in price

    (d) Responsiveness of demand for a commodity for a percentage change in its price

Answer (b) Percentage change in one variable in response to one percent change in another variable.

Question 11. When quantity demanded falls more than proportionally in response to price increase, then demand is

    (a) unitary elastic

    (b) perfectly inelastic

    (c) elastic

    (d) inelastic

Answer (c) elastic

Question 12. Fill the correct value of elasticity marked against the different points marked on the demand curve

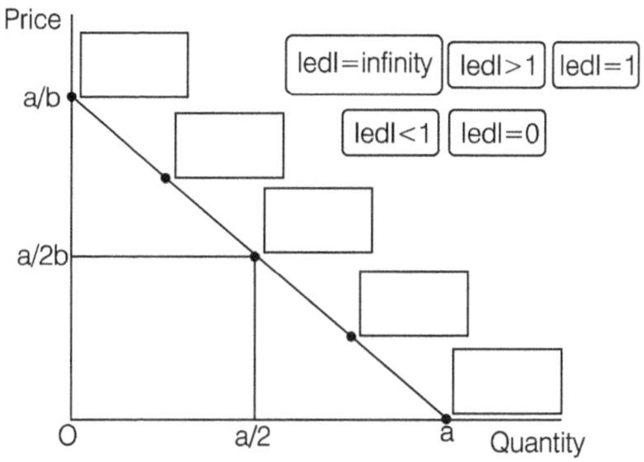

Answer ed=infinity , ed>1, ed=1, ed<1, ed=0

Question 13. Quantity of goods and services that people are willing to buy for a particular price and at a particular point of time is called?

    (a) Quantity supplied   (b) Budget line

    (c) Quantity demanded   (d) Law of demand

Answer (c) Quantity demanded

Question 14. Complementary goods are those goods which are used .... if price of one good increases, demand for its complementary will ....

    (a) together, constant

    (b) together, first increase then decrease

    (c) together, increase

    (d) together, decrease

Answer (d) together, decrease

Exercises

Question 1. What do you mean by the budget set of a consumer?

Answer Budget set is a set of all possible combinations of the set of two goods, which a consumer can afford at given price and income.

Question 2. What is budget line?

Answer Budget line represents different possible combinations of two goods which can be purchased by consumer with given income and prices, and the cost of each of these combinations is equal to the income of consumer.

Question 3. Explain why the budget line is downward sloping.

Answer The budget line is downward sloping because when more and more units of one good can be bought, it leads to decrease some units of other good with the given income.

Question 4. A consumer wants to consume two goods. The prices of two goods are ₹ 4 and ₹ 5 respectively. The consumer's income is ₹ 20.

   (i) Write down the equation of budget line.
  (ii) How much of good 1 can the consumer consume if she spends her entire income on that good?
 (iii) How much of good 2 can she consume if she spends her entire income on that good?
  (iv) What is the slope of the budget line?

Answer (i) Assume

$$\text{Good 1 be } X, \text{ Good 2 be } Y$$

Given,

Price of $X = $ ₹ 4 $(P = ₹\,4)$

Price of $Y = $ ₹ 5 $(P = ₹\,5)$

Income of the consumer $= $ ₹ 20

$\because$ Budget line $\Rightarrow P_x + P_y = $ Income

$\therefore$ Budget line will be $4X + 5Y = 20$

$\because$ Budget line $= $ Money spent $= $ Income

  (ii) If she spends her entire income on good 1 (X) then the consumption of good 2 (Y) will be zero.

Budget line $= P_x + P_y = $ Income (from (i))

$$\therefore \quad 4X + 5(0) = 20$$

$$X = \frac{20}{4} = 5 \text{ units}$$

(iii) If she spends her entire income on good 2 (Y), then the consumption of good 1 (X) will be zero.

Budget line $= P_x + P_y =$ Income (from (i))

$$\therefore \qquad 4(0) + 5Y = 20$$

$$Y = \frac{20}{5} = 4 \text{ units}$$

(iv) Slope of budget line $= \dfrac{\text{Units of good 1 willing to sacrifice}}{\text{Units of good 2 willing to gain}}$

$$= \frac{-\Delta P_x}{\Delta P_y}$$

$$= \frac{-4}{5} = -0.8$$

Note Sacrificed units always have negative value.

Questions 5, 6 and 7 are related to question 4.

Question 5. How does the budget line change, if the consumer's income increases to ₹ 40 but the prices remain unchanged?

Answer If consumer's income increases to ₹ 40, then consumer can buy more of both the goods (combination goods). It will shift the budget line upward right from AB to A_1, B_1, but new budget line will be parallel to the old budget line as there is no change in slope of budget line.

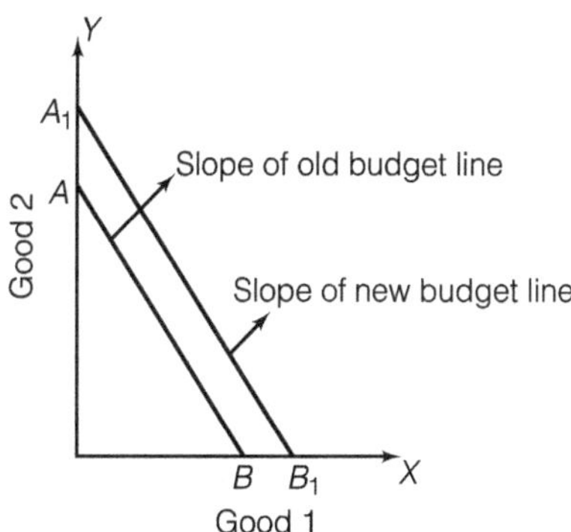

Question 6. How does the budget line change, if the price of good 2 decreases by a rupee but the price of good 1 and the consumer's income remain unchanged?

Answer If the price of good 2 decreases and the price of good 1 and income of consumer remain unchanged, then the budget line will be

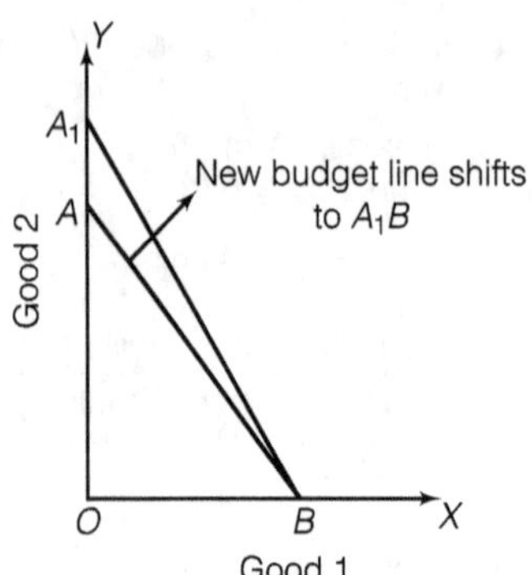

In above figure, budget line shift to the right from AB to A_1B only on Y - axis but unchanged on X-axis (because there is no change in the price of good1).

Question 7. What happens to the budget set, if both the prices as well as the income double?

Answer There will be no change in the budget set.

Explanation by Example.

Let,

Price of good 1 $(X) = ₹\, 2$

Price of good 2 $(Y) = ₹\, 4$

Income of consumer $= ₹\, 50$

Budget line will be $\Rightarrow$ $2X + 4Y = 50$

if prices as well as the income doubles, then new budget line will be

$$\Rightarrow \qquad\qquad 4X + 8Y = 100$$

$$\Rightarrow \qquad\qquad 2\,(2X + 4Y) = 2\,(50)$$

$$\Rightarrow \qquad\qquad 2X + 4Y = 50$$

Therefore, there will be no change in the budget set.

Question 8. Suppose a consumer can afford to buy 6 units of good 1 and 8 units of good 2, if she spends her entire income. The prices of the two goods are ₹ 6 and ₹ 8 respectively. How much is the consumer's income?

Answer Assume,

Good 1 $= X$, Good 2 $= Y$

Price of $X = P_x$, Price of $Y = P_y$

Income $= M$

Budget line is $P_x X + P_y Y = M$

After the putting value, we get
$$6 \times 6 + 8 \times 8 = M$$
$$\text{Income } (M) = 100$$

where, $X = 6$ units; $P_x = ₹ 6$; $Y = 8$ unit ; $P_y = ₹ 8$

Question 9. Suppose a consumer wants to consume two goods which are available only in integer units. The two goods are equally priced at ₹ 10 and the consumer's income is ₹ 40.

(i) Write down all the bundles that are available to the consumer.

(ii) Among the bundles that are available to the consumer, identify those which cost her exactly ₹ 40.

Answer (i) Given,

Price of goods (P_1) and good $2 = ₹10$

Income of consumer $= ₹ 40$

The bundles are available to the consumer -

First option - (0,0), (0,1), (0,2), (0,3), (0,4)

Second option - (1,0), (1,1), (1,2), (1,3)

Third option - (2,0), (2,1), (2,2)

Fourth option - (3,0), (3,1)

Fifth option - (4,0)

(ii) The exactly cost of ₹ 40, the bundles are

(0,4), (1,3), (2,2), (3,1) and (4,0)

Explanation

(a) First bundle (0,4)
Cost $= 0 \times 10 + 4 \times 10 = ₹ 40$

(b) Second bundle (1,3)
Cost $= 1 \times 10 + 3 \times 10 = 10 + 30 = ₹ 40$

(c) Fifth bundle (4,0)
Cost $= 4 \times 10 + 0 \times 10 = ₹ 40$

Question 10. What do you mean by 'monotonic preferences'?

Answer It means greater consumption of a commodity by the consumer gives higher level of satisfaction.

Question 11. If a consumer has monotonic preferences, can she be indifferent between the bundles (10,8) and (8,6)?

Answer The bundle (10,8) should be preferred instead of bundle (8,6) because bundle (10,8) has more of both goods.

Question 12. Suppose a consumer's preferences are monotonic. What can you say about her preference ranking over the bundles (10,10), (10,9) and (9,9)?

Answer A consumer's preferences will rank as

Rank 1st - (10,10)

Rank 2nd - (10,9)

Rank 3rd - (9,9)

Rank based on monotonic preferences.

Question 13. Suppose your friend is indifferent to the bundles (5,6) and (6,6). Are preferences of your friend monotonic?

Answer The preferences is monotonic because his bundles shows the more goods to less goods and monotonic preference implies more and more consumption of two sets of goods to get maximum satisfaction.

Question 14. Suppose there are two consumers in the market for a goods and their demand functions are as follows

$d_1(p) = 20 - p$ for any price less than or equal to 20 and $d_1(p) = 0$ at any price greater than 20

$d_2(p) = 30 - 2p$ for any price less than or equal to 15 and $d_1(P) = 0$ at any price greater than 15.

Find out is the market demand function.

Answer In the given demand functions, both the consumers do not want to demand the goods for any price above ₹ 15. Both of them demand only at a price less than or equal to ₹ 15. Therefore, market demand will be

$$(p) = d_1(p) + d_2(p)$$
$$(p) = 20 - p + 30 - 2p$$
$$(p) = 50 - 3p$$

For any price less than or equal to 15 and market demand $(p) = 0$ at any price greater than 15.

Question 15. Suppose there are 20 consumers for a good they have identical demand functions $d(p) = 10 - 3p$ for any price less than or equal to 10/3 and $d_1(P) = 0$ at any price greater than 10/3, what is the market demand function?

Answer In the given demand function, if the consumers demand only when price is either less than or equal to 10/3. Therefore, market demand will be

(d) Market demand

$$(p) = 20[d(p)]$$
$$(p) = 20(10 - 3p)$$
$$(p) = 200 - 60p$$

For any price less than or equal to 10/3 and market $(p) = 0$ at any price greater than 10/3.

Question 16. Consider a market where there are just two consumers and suppose their demands for goods are given as follows

P	d_1	d_2
1	9	24
2	8	20
3	7	18
4	6	16
5	5	14
6	4	12

Calculate the market demand for the good.

Answer

Price (₹)	Demand (d_1)	Demand (d_2)	Market Demand $(d_1 + d_2)$
1	9	24	33
2	8	20	28
3	7	18	25
4	6	16	22
5	5	14	19
6	4	12	16

Question 17. What do you mean by a normal good?

Answer   Normal goods refer to those goods whose demand increases with an increase in income. *e.g.,* When income increases, the demand of "Sugar" is also increases. Thus "Sugar" is a normal good.

Question 18. What do you mean by an 'inferior good'? Give some examples.

Answer   Inferior goods refer to those goods whose demand decreases with an increase in income. *e.g.,* If demand of Jaggery decreases with increase in income, then Jaggery is an inferior good.

Question 19. What do you mean by substitutes? Give examples of two goods which are substitutes of each other.

Answer Substitutes refer to those goods which can be used in place of another good for satisfaction of a particular want.

e.g., Pepsi and Coke, Coffee and Tea.

Question 20. What do mean by complements? Give examples of two goods which are complements of each other.

Answer Complements refer to those goods which are used together to satisfy a particular want. *e.g.,* Tea and Sugar, Car and Petrol.

Question 21. Explain price elasticity of demand.

Answer Price elasticity of demand refers to the percentage change in quantity demanded with reference to percentage change in price. It is measured in Ratio as

$$e_d = \frac{\% \text{ Change in Quantity demanded}}{\% \text{ Change in price}}$$

where, e_d =Price Elasticity of Demand

Question 22. Consider the demand for a good. At price ₹ 4, the demand for the good is 25 units. Suppose price of good increases to ₹ 5 and as a result, the demand for the good falls to 20 units. Calculate the price elasticity.

Answer

$$P_0 = 4, \quad q_0 = 25, \quad P_1 = 5, \quad q_1 = 20, \quad \Delta p = 1, \quad \Delta q = -5$$

$$e_d = -\left(\frac{\Delta q}{\Delta P} \times \frac{P_0}{q_0}\right) = \frac{5}{1} \times \frac{4}{25} = 0.8$$

Question 23. Consider the demand curve $D(p) = 10 - 3p$. What is the elasticity at price $\frac{5}{3}$?

Answer Given,

Demand curve $D(p) = 10 - 3p$

Price $(p) = \dfrac{5}{3}$

$$e_d = -\frac{bp}{a - bp} = \frac{-3 \times \dfrac{5}{3}}{10 - 3 \times \dfrac{5}{3}} = \frac{-5}{5}$$

$$\therefore \qquad e_d = -1$$

Question 24. Suppose the price elasticity of demand for a good is -0.2. If there is a 5% increase in the price of good, by what percentage will the demand for the good go down?

Answer Given,

Change in price (increase) = 5 %

Elasticity of Demand $(e_d) = -0.2$

$$e_d = \frac{\% \text{ Change in Quantity demanded}}{\% \text{ Change in price}}$$

$$(-)\,0.2 = \frac{\% \text{ Change in Quantity demanded}}{5}$$

% Change in quantity demanded = -1 % (decrease)

Question 25. Suppose the price elasticity of demand for a good is -0.2. How will the expenditure on the good be affected if there is a 10% increase in the price of the goods?

Answer Total expenditure will rise if there is a 10% rise in the price of goods, since its demand is inelastic, *i.e.*, $e_d = -0.2$

Question 26. Suppose there was a 4% decrease in the price of a good and as a result, the expenditure on the good increased by 2%. What can you say about the elasticity of demand?

Answer The expenditure increases with a decrease in the price of good, this is the opposite change. Thus, the elasticity of demand is more than unit elastic *i.e.*, $(e_d > 1)$.

3

Production and Costs

Points to Remember

1. **Production** It is the transformation of resources into commodities.

2. **Production Function** Production function studies the functional relationship between physical input and physical output.

$$Y = F\,(L \cdot K)$$

Here, Y = Production, L = Labour, K = Capital

3. **Total Product** It is the sum total of output produced by all units of labour.

$$TP = AP \times L$$

Here, TP = Total product, AP = Product per unit of labour

L = Units of labour

4. **Marginal Product** It is the change in total production as a result of a unit change in input of a variable factor (ΔL)

ΔTP = Change in total production

$$MP = TP_n - TP_{n-1} \quad \text{or} \quad MP = \Delta TP / \Delta L$$

5. **Average Product** It is per unit production of the variable factor.

$$AP = TP / L$$

Here, AP = Average product; TP = Total product; L = Labour

6. **Short run** The time period during which a firm, in order to make changes in its production can change only in its variable factors but not in its fixed factor, is termed as short run.

7. **Long run** The time period in which a firm can change all the factors of production is termed as long run. In the long period, a firm can change its scale of plant also.

8. **Law of Diminishing Marginal Product** The law states that with the increase in variable factor, keeping all other factors constant the marginal product of the variable factor diminishes after a certain level of production.

   Reason for operating of law
   (i) Optimum combination
   (ii) Change in factor combinations

9. **Law of Variable Proportion** The law states that with the increase in a variable factor, keeping other factor constant, initially the marginal product rises but after reaching a certain level of employment it starts declining.

   Three stages of the law
   (i) Increasing returns   (ii) Diminishing returns
   (iii) Negative returns

10. **Returns to Scale** When producers change all the factors of production in the same production, the proportional relationship between output and factor inputs is known as returns to scale.
    (i) **Constant Returns to Scale** When a proportional increase in all inputs results in an increase in output by the same proportion is called constant returns to scale.
    (ii) **Increasing Returns to Scale** IRS holds when proportional increase in all inputs results in an increase in output by more than the proportion.
    (iii) **Decreasing Returns to Scale** DRS holds when proportional in all inputs results in an increase in output by less than the proportion.

11. **Cost Function** The functional relationship between cost and quantity produced is termed as cost function.

    $$C = F(Q_x)$$

    Here, C = Production – Cost; Q_x = Quantity produced of x goods

12. **Cost of Production** Cost is the expenditure incurred by the producers on purchase of factor inputs such as land, labour capital etc, non-factor inputs such as raw material, fuel etc.

13. **Explicit Cost** The cost of those inputs whose payment is made to outsider of the firm. It is an accounting cost.

14. **Implicit Cost** The cost of self owned inputs used in the production process is called implicit cost.

    e.g., rent of ownland, interest of own implicit etc.

15. **Total Cost** (TC)   It is the sum total of fixed cost and variable cost corresponding to a given level of output.

$$TC = TFC + TVC$$

Here,   TFC = Total Fixed Cost

TVC = Total Variable Cost;   TC = Total Cost

16. **Total Fixed Cost** (TFC)   TFC are the costs that are incurred on fixed factor inputs and do not vary with the output.

e.g.,   Rent of factory, Interest on bonds,

$$TFC = \text{Quantities of the fixed productive services} \times \text{Factor price}$$

or $TFC = TC - TVC$

17. **Total Variable Cost**   The costs that are incurred on variable factor inputs and very directly with the output are called total variable costs.

e.g.,   Raw material, fuel, electric power.

$$TVC = \text{Quantities of the variable productive service} \times \text{Factor price}$$

or $TVC = TC - TFC$

18. **Average Cost** (AC)   Average cost is the cost per unit of output produced.

$$AC = TC / Q ; \qquad Q = \text{Units of output}$$

$$AC = AFC + AVC$$

AFC = Average Fixed Cost

AVC = Average Variable Cost

19. **Average Fixed Cost**   Total fixed cost per unit of output incurred to a firm may be defined as average fixed cost.

$$AFC = \frac{TFC}{Q}$$

20. **Averages Variable Cost** (AVC)   Total variable cost per unit of output incurred to a firm is defined as the average variable cost.

$$AFC = \frac{TVC}{Q}$$

21. **Marginal Cost** (MC)   It is the additional cost owing to the production of an additional unit of output.

$$MC_n = TC_n - TC_{n-1}$$

Since additional cost can only be variable cost.

22. **Shape of Curves**
    (i) AC, AVC, MC curve U shaped due to law of returns to factor.
    (ii) TFC curve straight line $\parallel$ to X-axis.
    (iii) TC and TVC curve upward sloping.
    (iv) AFC curve downward rectangular hyperbola.

QR Code Questions

Question 1. In the Cobb-Douglas production function, when the sum of coefficients a+b=1, then it is called constant returns to scale.

   (a) True   (b) False

Answer (a) True

Question 2. Law of Variable Proportion states that if we keep increasing one factor, keeping other factors constant, then the Marginal Product of that factor will increase.

   (a) True   (b) False

Answer (b) Law of Variable Proportion states that if we keep increasing one factor, keeping other factors constant, then the Marginal Product of that factor will reduce.

Question 3. Fill in the missing word

In case of giffen goods, the relationship between price and demand for a quantity is .... (Positive/Negative).

Answer Positive

   This concept is explained in Chapter-2 (Part-A) of NCERT Book.

Question 4. When Marginal Product and Average Product both are increasing, then

   (a) Marginal Product will increase at a lesser rate than Average Product.
   (b) Marginal Product will increase at a greater rate than Average Product.
   (c) Average Product will increase at a constant rate.
   (d) Average Product will increase at a greater rate than Marginal Product.

Answer (b) Marginal Product will increase at a greater rate than Average Product.

Question 5. .... is the cost of factors in its next best alternative use

    (a) Fixed cost   (b) Opportunity cost
    (c) Marginal cost   (d) Average cost

Answer (b) Opportunity cost

       This concept is explained in Chapter-1 (Part-A) of NCERT Book.

Question 6. Productive contribution of humans who work is called ....

    (a) Land   (b) Machine
    (c) Labour   (d) Capital

Answer (c) Labour

Question 7. The law of diminishing returns being at the level of output where

    (a) Marginal cost is at a minimum
    (b) Average variable cost is at a minimum
    (c) Total cost is at maximum
    (d) Average fixed cost is at minimum

Answer (a) Marginal cost is at a minimum

Question 8. Which of the following is variable cost?

    (a) Interest Payment   (b) Property taxes
    (c) Raw material costs   (d) All of these

Answer (c) Raw material costs

Question 9. Improvement in technology causes

    (a) Decrease in quantity supplied   (b) Decrease in supply
    (c) Increase in supply
    (d) Increase in quantity demanded

Answer (c) Increase in supply

       This concept is explained in Chapter-5 (Part-A) of NCERT Book.

Question 10. Net profit is

    (a) TR-TFC-TVC   (b) TR-MC
    (c) TR-TVC   (d) TR-TFC

Answer (a) TR-TFC-TVC

       This concept is explained in Chapter-4 (Part-A) of NCERT Book.

Question 11. Return to scale are exhibited by
    (a) Long run production function
    (b) Both Long and Short Run Production Function
    (c) Short run production function
    (d) None of these

Answer (a) Long run production function

Question 12. Choose the correct words from the following

Total Product/Total Labour; Change in Output/Change in Input; Sum of total output produced; Fixed Factor

  (i) Total Product ....   (ii) Short Run ....
 (iii) Average Product .... (iv) Marginal Product ....

Answer (i) Sum of total output produced

     (ii) Fixed Factor

    (iii) Total Product/Total Labour

    (iv) Change in Output/Change in Input

Exercises

Question 1. Explain the concept of a production function.

Answer It is the technological knowledge that determines the maximum levels of output that can be produced using different combinations of inputs. If the technology improves, the maximum levels of output obtainable for different input combinations increase. Then we have a new production function.

e.g., A firm produce a product (Y) by using two inputs X_1 and X_2.

Then production function can be expressed as

$$q_y = f(X_1 . X_2)$$

Question 2. What is the total product of an input?

Answer Total product means the total quantity of goods produced by a firm during a given period of time with given inputs.

$$TP = AP \times \text{Number of variable factor } (L)$$

Question 3. What is the average product of an input?

Answer Average product is defined as the output produced per unit of variable input. Calculated as

$$AP = \frac{TP}{L}$$

Question 4. What is the marginal product of an input?

Answer   Marginal product refers to the additional output produced, when one more unit of variable factor is employed.

Calculated as

$$MP = \frac{\text{Change in output}}{\text{Change in input}} = \frac{\Delta q}{\Delta X_1}$$

Question 5. Explain the relationship between the marginal products and the total product of an input.

Answer

Units of Fixed Factor	Units of Variable Factor	MP	TP	AP
1	0	–	0	–
1	1	6	6	6
1	2	14	20	10
1	3	28	48	16
1	4	24	72	18
1	5	8	80	16
1	6	4	84	14
1	7	0	84	12
1	8	– 2	80	0

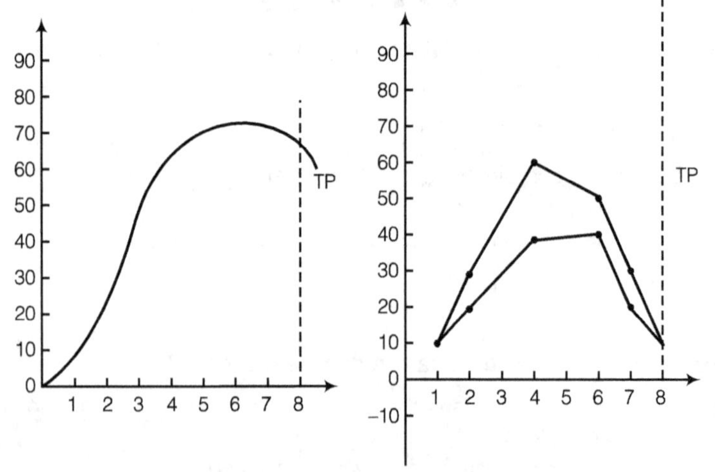

Relation between TP and MP

   (i) When MP increases, TP increases at increasing rate.

   (ii) When MP starts diminishing, TP increases only at diminishing rate.

   (iii) When MP = 0, TP is maximum.

   (iv) When MP is negative, TP is declining.

Question 6. Explain the concepts of the short run and the long run.

Answer **Short run** Short run refers to a period in which output can be changed by changing only variable factors.

In the short run, fixed inputs like land, building, plant machinery etc, cannot be changed. It means, production can be raised by increasing only variable factors, but till the extent of fixed factors.

Long run Long run refers to a period in which output can be changed by changing all factors of production. In the long run, firm can change its factory size, techniques of production, purchase new plant machinery, patents etc.

Question 7. What is the law of diminishing marginal product?

Answer Law of diminishing marginal product means that when more and more units of a variable factors are employed along with a fixed factor, the marginal product of the factor must fall. *e.g.,*

Units of Fixed Factor	Units of Variable Factor	MP
1	0	–
1	1	6
1	2	16
1	3	28
1	4	20
1	5	8
1	6	2
1	7	0
1	8	−2

Question 8. What is law of variable proportions?

Answer The law which exhibits the relationship between the units of a variable factor (Keeping all other factors constant) and the amount of output in the short-run known as law of variable proportion.

Question 9. When does a production function satisfy constant returns to scale?

Answer Production function satisfy constant returns, when MP becomes zero and TP reaches its maximum point.

Question 10. When does a production function satisfy increasing returns to scale?

Answer A production function satisfy increasing returns, when every additional variable factor adds more and more to the total output. It means TP increase at an increasing order and MP also increases.

Question 11. When does a production function satisfy decreasing returns to scale?

Answer A production function satisfy decreasing returns, when every additional variable factor adds lesser and lesser amount of output. It means TP increases at a diminishing rate and MP falls with increase in variable factor.

Question 12. Briefly explain the concept of the cost function.

Answer **Cost Function** The functional relationship between cost and quantity produced is termed as cost function.

$C = F(Q_x)$; C = Production Cost; Q_x = Quantity produced of $\times$ goods.

Cost function of a firm depends on two things.

   (i) Production function,

   (ii) Price of the factors of production. Higher the output of a firm, higher would be the production cost. That's why it depends on quantum of output.

Question 13. What are the total fixed cost, total variable cost and total cost of a firm? How are they related?

Answer **Total Fixed Cost** The cost which does not change with the change in output. Even when output is zero.

In other words, fixed costs are the sum total expenditure on the purchase or hiring of fixed factors of production.

Total Variable Cost The cost which change with the change in output.

In other words, variable costs are the expenditure incurred on the use of variable factors of production.

Total Cost Total cost is the sum total of total fixed cost and total variable cost at various level of output.

Relation among TFC, TVC and TC

Cost Schedule Table

Output (Units)	TFC	TVC	TC = TFC + TVC
0	15	0	15+0=15
1	15	5	15+5=20
2	15	12	15+12=27
3	15	20	15+20=35
4	15	28	15+28=43
5	15	35	15+35=50
6	15	42	15+42=67

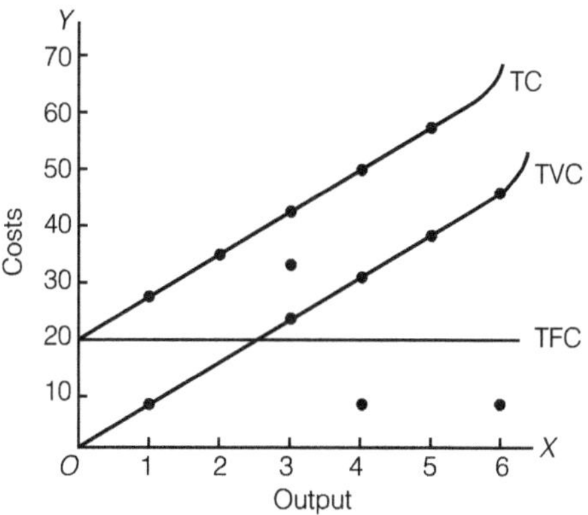

(i) TC = TFC = TVC.

(ii) TFC is constant at all levels of output.

(iii) TVC increases as output increases.

(iv) TC is parallel to TVC.

Question 14. What are the average fixed cost, average variable cost and average cost of a firm? How are they related?

Answer

(i) **Average Fixed Cost** (AFC) It refers to the per unit fixed cost of production.

Calculated as

$$AFC = \frac{TFC}{Q}$$

where TFC = Total Fixed Cost; Q = Quantity of output

(ii) **Average Variable Cost** (AVC) It refers to the per unit variable cost of production. Calculated as

$$AVC = \frac{TVC}{Q}$$

where TVC = Total Variable Cost; Q = Quantity of output

(iii) **Average Cost** (AC) It refers to the per unit total cost of production.

Calculated as

$$AC = \frac{TC}{Q}$$

where TC = Total Cost
Q = Quantity of output

Show Curve Before Relations

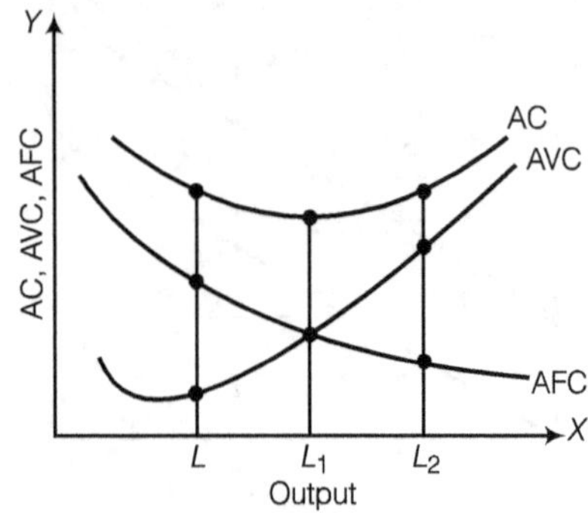

Relation of AFC, AVC and AC

(i) AC = AFC + AVC.

(ii) AC and AVC can never be equal for any level of output.

(iii) AFC is never zero as TFC is fixed at all levels of output.

(iv) AFC must fall because TFC is constant.

(v) The curves of AC and AVC never intersect.

Question 15. Can there be some fixed cost in the long run? If not, why?

Answer No, there are no fixed costs in the long-run as all the factors are variable. Fixed cost exists only in the short run.

Question 16. What does the average fixed cost curve look like? Why does it look so?

Answer The average fixed cost curve looks like a rectangular hyperbola. It happens because same amount of fixed cost is divided by increasing output. As a result, AFC curve slope downwards and is a rectangular hyperbola.

Question 17. What do the short run marginal cost, average variable cost and short run average cost curves look like?

Answer The curves of short-run marginal cost, average variable cost and average cost are U shaped.

Question 18. Why does the SMC curve cut the AVC curve at the minimum point of the AVC curve?

Answer It is only when AVC is constant and at its minimum point, that SMC is equal to AVC. Therefore, SMC curve cuts AVC curve at its minimum points. And when AVC falls, SMC is less than AVC.

Question 19. At which point does the SMC curve cut the SAC curve? Give reason in support of your answer.

Answer SMC curve cuts the SAC curve at its minimum point. It happens because when SAC falls. SMC is less than SAC. When SAC starts rising ; SMC is more than SAC. It is only when SAC is constant and at its minimum point.

Question 20. Why is the short run marginal cost curve U-shaped?

Answer Short-run marginal cost curve is U-shaped because of the law of variable proportions. In the short run as the employment of variable factor increases (fixed factor being constant) in the initial stage MC decreases owing to increasing return but finally tend to rise in accordance with the law of variable proportion. Hence the U-shape of MC.

Question 21. What do the long run marginal cost and the average cost curves look like?

Answer Long run marginal cost and the average costs curve is U shaped but fallter than shortrun U-shaped.

Question 22. The following table gives the total product schedule of labour. Find the corresponding average product and marginal product schedules of labour.

L	0	1	2	3	4	5
TP_L (Units)	0	15	35	50	40	48

Answer

Labour (L)	TP (Units)	$AP = \dfrac{TP}{L}$	$MP = TP_n - TP_{n-1}$
0	0	–	–
1	15	15.00	$15 - 0 = 15$
2	35	17.50	$35 - 15 = 20$
3	50	16.67	$50 - 35 = 15$
4	40	10.00	$40 - 50 = -10$
5	48	9.60	$40 - 48 = -8$

Question 23. The following table gives the average product schedule of labour. Find the total product and marginal product schedules. It is given that the total product is zero at zero level of labour employment.

L	1	2	3	4	5	6
AP_L	2	3	4	4.25	4	3.5

Answer

Labour (L)	AP_L	$TP = AP_L \times L$	$MP = TP_n - TP_{n-1}$
1	2.00	2	2
2	3.00	6	$6 - 2 = 4$
3	4.00	12	$12 - 6 = 6$
4	4.25	17	$17 - 12 = 5$
5	4.00	20	$20 - 17 = 3$
6	3.5.0	21	$21 - 20 = 1$

$$AP = \frac{TP}{L} \quad \therefore \quad TP = AP \times L$$

Question 24. The following table gives the marginal product schedule of labour. It is also given that total product of labour is zero at zero level of employment. Calculate the total and average product schedules of labour.

L	1	2	3	4	5	6
MP_L	3	5	7	5	3	1

Answer

Labour (L)	MP of Labour (Units)	TP (Units)	AP (Units); $AP = \dfrac{TP}{L}$
1	3	3	3
2	5	$3 + 5 = 8$	4
3	7	$8 + 7 = 15$	5
4	5	$15 + 5 = 20$	5
5	3	$20 + 3 = 23$	4.60
6	1	$23 + 1 = 24$	4

Question 25. The following table shows the total cost schedule of a firm. What is the total fixed cost schedule of this firm? Calculate the TVC, AFC, AVC, SAC and SMC schedules of the firm.

Q	0	1	2	3	4	5	6
TC	10	30	45	55	70	90	120

Answer

Q (Units)	TC (₹)	TFC (₹)	$TVC = TC - TFC$	$SAC = \dfrac{TC}{Q}$	$SMC = TC_n - TC_{n-1}$
0	10	10	$10 - 10 = 0$	–	–
1	30	10	$30 - 10 = 20$	$30/1 = 30$	$30 - 10 = 20$
2	45	10	$45 - 10 = 35$	$45/2 = 22.5$	$45 - 30 = 15$
3	55	10	45	18.33	$55 - 45 = 10$
4	70	10	60	17.50	15
5	90	10	80	18	20
6	120	10	110	20	30

$AFC = \dfrac{TFC}{Q}$	$AVC = \dfrac{TVC}{Q}$
–	–
$10/1 = 10$	$20/1 = 20$
$10/2 = 5$	$35/2 = 17.50$
$10/3 = 3.33$	$45/3 = 15$
$10/4 = 2.50$	$60/4 = 15$
$10/5 = 2$	$80/5 = 16$
$10/6 = 1.67$	$110/6 = 18.33$

Here,

Q = Output in Units; TC = Total Cost

TFC = Total Factor Cost (Fixed); TVC = Total Variable Cost

SAC = Short run Average Cost or AC

SMC = Short run Marginal Cost or MC

AFC = Average Factor Cost (Fixed)

AVC = Average Variable Cost

Question 26. The following table gives the total cost schedule of a firm. It is also given that the average fixed cost at 4 units of output is ₹ 5. Find the TVC, TFC, AVC, AFC, SAC and SMC schedules of the firm for the corresponding values of output.

Q	1	2	3	4	5	6
TC	50	65	75	95	130	185

Answer

Q (Units)	TC (₹)	$TFC = U \times S$	$TVC =$ $TC - TFC$	SAC $= \dfrac{TC}{Q}$	SMC $= TC_n - TC_{n-1}$	AFC $= \dfrac{TFC}{Q}$	AVC $= \dfrac{TVC}{Q}$
1	50	20	30	50	30	20	30
2	65	20	45	32.5	15	10	22.50
3	75	20	55	25	10	6.67	18.33
4	95	20	75	23.75	20	5	18.75
5	130	20	110	26.0	35	4	22
6	185	20	165	30.83	55	3.33	27.50

Question 27. A firm's SMC schedule is shown in the following table. The total fixed cost of the firm is ₹ 100. Find the TVC, TC, AVC and SAC schedules of the firm.

Q	0	1	2	3	4	5	6
TC	–	500	300	200	300	500	800

Answer

Q (Units)	TC	TFC	TVC = ΣMC	TC = FC + VC	AVC = $\dfrac{TVC}{Q}$	SAC = $\dfrac{TC}{Q}$
0	–	100	0	100	–	–
1	500	100	500	600	500	600
2	300	100	500 + 300 = 800	900	400	450
3	200	100	800 + 200 = 1000	1100	333.33	366.67
4	300	100	1000 + 300 = 1300	1400	325	350
5	500	100	1800	1900	360	380
6	800	100	2600	2700	433.33	450

Question 28. Let the production function of a firm be $Q = 5, L^{1/2} K^{1/2}$. Find out the maximum possible output that the firm can produce with 100 units of L and 100 units of K.

Answer   Given $Q = 5$, $L = 100$ units, $K = 100$ units

$$\because \qquad Q_x = F(X_1 \cdot X_2) \text{ (Production function equation)}$$

After putting values $Q_x = 5 \cdot 100^{1/2} \cdot 100^{1/2} = 5\sqrt{100} \cdot \sqrt{100} = 500$

$\therefore$ Maximum output = 500 units

Question 29. Let the production function of a firm be $Q = 2L^2 K^2$. Find out the maximum possible output that the firm can produce with 5 units of L and 2 units of K. What is the maximum possible output that the firm can produce with zero unit of L and 10 units of K ?

Answer   Given, $Q = 2L^2 K^2$, $L = 5$ units, $K = 2$ units,

$$\because \qquad Q_x = f(X_1 . X_2)$$

After putting given values $Q = 2\,(5)^2 (2)^2 = 200$ units

Maximum possible output with 0 unit of L and 10 units of K

Again putting new values in equation $Q = 2(0)^2 (10)^2 = 0$ units

Question 30. Find out the maximum possible output for a firm with zero unit of L and 10 units of K when its production function is $Q = 5L + 2K$

Answer Given $Q = 5L + 2K$, $L = 0$ units, $K = 10$ units

After putting values in equation

$$Q = 5(0) + 2(10) = 20 \text{ units}$$

$\therefore$ The maximum output = 20 units.

4

The Theory of the Firm Under Perfect Competition

Points to Remember

1. **Perfect Competition** A market in which we find perfect competition between a large number of buyers and a large number of sellers of a homogeneous product and uniform price is called perfect competition market.

2. **Features of Perfect Competition**
   (i) Large number of buyers and sellers
   (ii) Homogeneous product
   (iii) Freedom of entry or exit
   (iv) Perfect mobility   (v) Perfect knowledge

3. **Price Line** The line plotted for different values of output in the output price plane is called price line.

   In perfect competitive market for an individual firm price line and demand curve are same.

4. **Revenue** It refers to the money receipts of a firm from the sale of its output.

5. **Total Revenue** (TR) It is the sum total of revenue derived from the sale of all units of the commodity.

$$TR = P \times Q \quad \text{or} \quad AR \times Q$$

or $\quad \Sigma MR$

Here, $\quad P = \text{Price}, Q = \text{Output}$

$AR = \text{Average revenue}, MR = \text{Marginal Revenue}$

6. **Average Revenue** It is the revenue per unit output sold

$$AR = \frac{TR}{Q}$$

7. **Marginal Revenue**: It is the change in total revenue as a result of selling one more (or less) unit of output.

$$MR = TR_n - TR_{n-1} \quad \text{or} \quad MR = \frac{\Delta TR}{\Delta Q}$$

Δ = Any change

8. **Shape of TR, AR, MR, curves in Perfect Competition**
    (i) Under Perfect Competition TR curve in an upward slopping straight line starting from the origin.
    (ii) Under Perfect Competition AR and MR curve is same and $\parallel$ to X-axis.

9. **Profit** It is the difference between revenue and cost.

$$\text{Profit} = (\pi) = \text{Revenue} - \text{Cost}$$

10. **Break Even Point** Break even for a firm occurs when it is able to cover its all costs of production.

    Accordingly, break- even point is defined as a situation when

$$TR = TC \quad \text{or} \quad AR = AC$$

    Under this situation, the firm earns only normal profits.

11. **Shutdown Point** It occurs when firm is just able to cover its variable costs, increasing the loss of fixed cost of production.

    Accordingly shut down point is defined as a situation when

$$TR = TVC \quad \text{or} \quad AR = AVC$$

12. **Producer Equilibrium or Profit Maximisation** A producer is said to be in equilibrium, when he maximises his profits or minimises his losses.

    Condition of profit maximisation
    (i) $MR = MC$
    (ii) MC is rising or MC should cut MR from below.

13. **Profit Maximisation in the Short-run under Perfect Competition**
    - Condition-1, $MR = MC$ or $AR = P$
    - Condition-2, MC curve should cut the $MR = AR$ curve from below
    - Condition-3, $P \geq AVC$

14. **Meaning of Supply** Supply means the amount of a commodity that firms are able and willing to offer for sale in the market in a given period of time and at a given price.

15. **Supply Schedule** Tabular statements of relationship between price and supply of commodity is called supply schedule.

16. **Supply Curve** Graphical presentation of relationship between price and supply of a commodity is called supply curve.

17. **Market Supply Curve** The market supply curve for a commodity shows relationship between the price of a given commodity and quantity sellers are inclined to sell.

18. **Determinant of Supply Curve**
  (i) Technological progress
  (ii) Input price
  (iii) Unit tax

19. **Short-run Supply Curve** The supply curve of a firm tells us the quantity of the product that a profit maximising firm is willing to produce at each possible price.

20. **Elasticity of Supply** It can be defined as a measure of the degree of responsiveness of quantity supplied to changes in the commodity's own prices.

21. **Measurement of Elasticity of Supply**

Percentage method

$$E_s = \frac{\text{\% Change in quantity supplied}}{\text{\% Change in price}} \quad \text{or} \quad \frac{\Delta Q}{\Delta P} = \frac{P}{Q}$$

Here, P = Actual Price, Q = Actual Quantity

ΔP = Change in Price, ΔQ = Change in Quantity

22. **Two Extreme Cases of Elasticity of Supply**
  (i) Perfect elastic supply ($e_s = \infty$)
  (ii) Perfect inelastic supply ($e_s = 0$)

QR Code Question

Question 1. Homogeneous product is a characteristic of
  (a) perfect competition only
  (b) both perfect competition and oligopoly
  (c) monopoly
  (d) perfect oligopoly only

Answer (b) both perfect competition and oligopoly

Exercises

Question 1. What are the characteristics of a perfectly competitive market?

Answer The main characteristics of a perfectly competitive market are as follows

   (i) Large number of buyers and sellers.
   (ii) Homogeneous goods.
   (iii) Free entry and exit of firms.
   (iv) Buyers and sellers have perfect knowledge of market.
   (v) Perfect mobility of factors of production.
   (vi) The transportation costs assumed zero.
   (vii) There is no selling costs.

Question 2. How are the total revenue of a firm, market price and the quantity sold by the firm related to each other?

Answer Total Revenue is the sum total of revenue receipts from the sale of a given quantity of a commodity.

It means total revenue is obtained by multiplying the market price (sale price) of commodity and quantity of the commodity sold.

Total Revenue = Market price × Quantity sold

Question 3. What is the 'price line'?

Answer It is a horizontal line that represents the market price for a perfectly competitive firm and output. Under monopoly of monopolistic competition, firm price line slope downward. For a perfectly competitive firm, price line and demand curve are same.

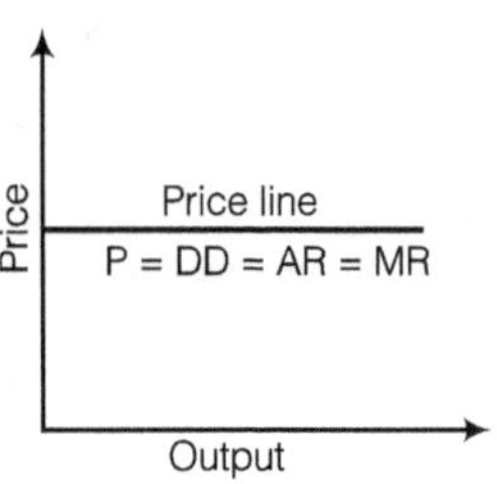

Question 4. Why is the total revenue curve of a price-taking firm an upward sloping straight line? Why does the curve pass through the origin?

Answer For a price taking firm, AR is constant. In case AR is constant, MR is also constant. As a result TR increases in the same proportion as price is constant. So, TR curve is upward sloping straight line. It passes from the origin because TR is zero at zero level of output.

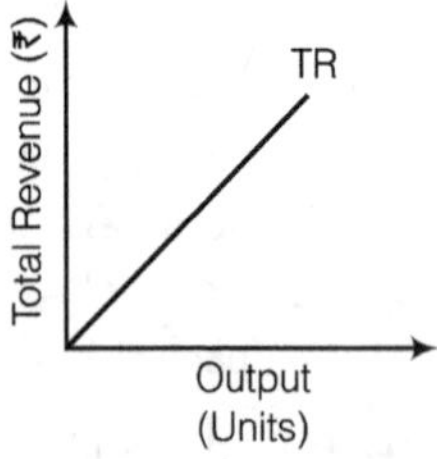

Question 5. What is the relation between market price and average revenue of a price-taking firm?

Answer   For a price taking firm, market price is equal to average revenue. We know,

$$AR = \frac{TR}{Q}$$

$$TR = P \times Q ; \quad AR = \frac{P \times Q}{Q}$$

So, $AR = P$

Here   AR = Average Revenue

TR = Total Revenue

Question 6. What is relation between market price and marginal revenue of a price-taking firm?

Answer   For a price taking firm, market price is equal to marginal revenue because firm can sell more quantity of commodity at the same price. As a result that revenue from every additional unit (MR) is equal to price or average revenue AR.

Question 7. What conditions must hold if a profit maximising firm produces positive output in a competitive market?

Answer   When price remains constant, firms can sell any quantity of output at the price fixed by the market. AR remains same at all levels of output and also revenue from every additional unit (MR) is equal to AR. It means, AR curve is same as MR curve.

Producer aims to produce that level of output at which MC is equal to MR and MC is greater than MR after MC = MR output level.

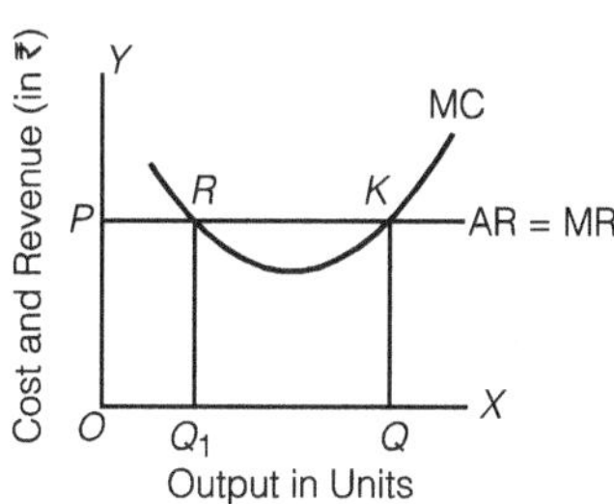

Output in Units
Producer's Equilibrium (MR – MC)
(When price remains constant)

Question 8. Can there be a positive level of output that a profit maximising firm produces in a competitive market at which market price is not equal to marginal cost? Give an explanation.

Answer　No, because it is not possible as equality between market price and marginal cost is a necessary condition for perfectly competitive firm to be in equilibrium. Only when price remain constant at all output levels, the market price is equal to marginal revenue in case of perfect competition.

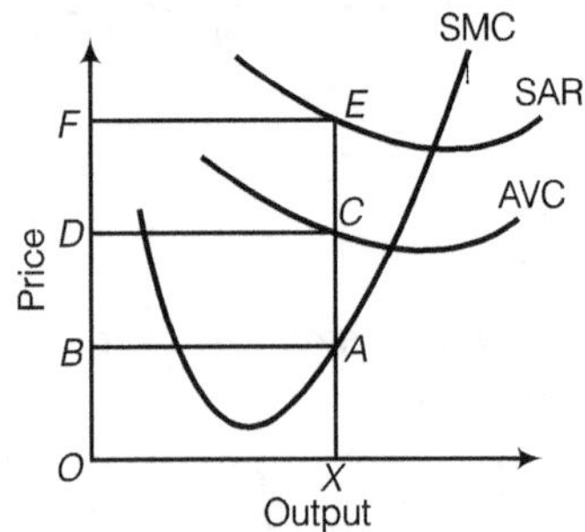

Question 9. Will a profit maximising firm in a competitive market ever produce a positive level of output in the range where the marginal cost is falling? Give an explanation.

Answer　No, because the essential condition of producer's equilibrium is that marginal cost curve should be rising. So, a profit maximising firm will produce that quantity of output at which its MC is rising and not falling.

Question 10. Will a profit maximising firm in a competitive market produce a positive level of output in the short-run if the market price is less than the minimum of AVC? Give an explanation.

Answer　No, a profit maximising firm will not produce a level of output in the short-run when market price is less than the minimum of AVC. It happens because equality between market price and minimum AVC indicates shut down point and a firm will never operate at a price less than the minimum AVC.

Question 11. Will a profit maximising firm in a competitive market produce a positive level of output in the long-run if the market price is less than the minimum of AC? Give an explanation.

Answer　No, it is not possible for a firm to produce positive level of output in the long-run, if the market price falls short of the minimum of AC. It is because in long-run there is free entry and exit of firms which leads to generate normal profit as their earning. Thus, any firm making loss in long-run stop the production.

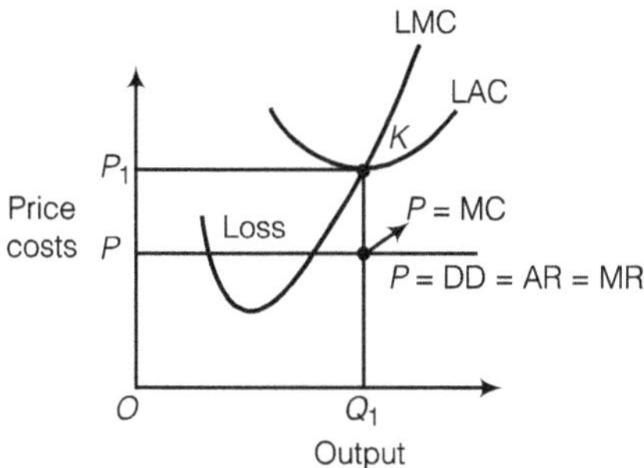

Question 12. What is the supply curve of a firm in the short-run?

Answer The supply curve of a firm in the short-run is less elastic and it is responsive to changes in price.

Question 13. What is the supply curve of a firm in the long-run?

Answer The supply curve of a firm in the long-run is highly elastic and it is more responsive to change in price.

Question 14. How does technological progress affect the supply curve of a firm?

Answer The technological progress affect the supply curve of a firm will shifts to downward (to the right). Because a firm can produce same level of output using less of inputs with improved technology. It causes fall to the marginal cost.

Question 15. How does the imposition of a unit tax affect the supply curve of a firm?

Answer A unit tax may be defined as the tax imposed by the government on per unit sale of output. The imposition of a unit tax shifts the marginal cost curve of the firm upward. Affect in supply curve will shift to the left.

Question 16. How does an increase in the price of an input affect the supply curve of a firm?

Answer An increase in the price of an input will affect marginal cost curve upward. So, supply curve shifts to the left. Therefore, an increase in the input price negatively affects the supply of the firm.

Question 17. How does an increase in the number of firms in a market affect the market supply curve?

Answer If number of firms increase in a market, the market supply curve will shift to the right as there will be more number of firms supplying more amount of output.

Question 18. What does the price elasticity of supply mean? How do we measure it?

Answer The price elasticity of supply means the percentage change in quantity supplied caused by a given percentage change in price of commodity.

It is measured as

Price elasticity of supply $(E_s) = \dfrac{\text{Percentage change in quantity supplied}}{\text{Percentage change in price}}$

$$E_s = \frac{\Delta Q}{\Delta P} \times \frac{P}{Q}$$

ΔQ = change in supply

ΔP = change in price

P = initial price

Q = initial supply

Question 19. Compute the total revenue, marginal revenue and average revenue schedules in the following table. Market price of each unit of the good is ₹ 10.

Quantity Sold (Units)	TR (₹)	MR (₹)	AR (₹)
0	—	—	—
1	—	—	—
2	—	—	—
3	—	—	—
4	—	—	—
5	—	—	—
6	—	—	—

Answer

Quantity Sold (Units)	Price (P) (₹)	$TR = P \times Q$ (₹)	$AR = \dfrac{TR}{Q}$ (₹)	$MR = TR_n - TR_{n-1}$ (₹)
0	10	0	10	0
1	10	10	10	10
2	10	20	10	10
3	10	30	10	10
4	10	40	10	10
5	10	50	10	10
6	10	60	10	10

Question 20. The following table shows the total revenue and total cost schedules of a competitive firm. Calculate the profit at each output level. Determine also the market price of the good

Quantity Sold	0	1	2	3	4	5	6	7
TR (in ₹)	0	5	10	15	20	25	30	35
TC (in ₹)	5	7	10	12	15	23	33	40
Profit (in ₹)	—	—	—	—	—	—	—	—

Answer Profit = TR − TC

Profit (₹)	−5	−2	0	3	5	2	−3	−5

Market price $= \dfrac{TR}{Q}$

$i.e.,$ $\Rightarrow$ $\dfrac{5}{1} = 5$ ₹ at II stage

$\Rightarrow \dfrac{10}{2} = 5$ ₹ in III stage

and so on.

Question 21. The following table shows the total cost schedule of a competitive firm. It is given that the price of the good is ₹ 10. Calculate the profit at each output level. Find the profit maximising level of output.

Output	0	1	2	3	4	5	6	7	8	9	10
TC (₹)	5	15	22	27	31	38	49	63	81	101	123

Answer

Output	TC (₹)	Price (given)	TR = $Q \times P$	Profit = (TR − TC)
0	5	10	0	−5
1	15	10	10	−5
2	22	10	20	−2
3	27	10	30	3
4	31	10	40	9
5	38	10	50	12
6	49	10	60	11
7	63	10	70	7
8	81	10	80	−1
9	101	10	90	−11
10	123	10	100	−23

The profit maximising level at 5 units sold where firm is earning profit of ₹ 12.

Question 22. Consider a market with two firms. The following table shows the supply schedules of the two firms; the SS_1 column gives the supply schedule of firm 1 and the SS_2 column gives the supply schedule of firm 2. Compute the market supply schedule.

Price (₹)	0	1	2	3	4	5	6
SS_1 (Units)	0	0	0	1	2	3	4
SS_2 (Units)	0	0	0	1	2	3	4

Answer The market Supply Schedule

Price (₹)	SS_1 (Units)	SS_2 (Units)	Market Supply(SS_1+SS_2)
0	0	0	0
1	0	0	0
2	0	0	0
3	1	1	2
4	2	2	4
5	3	3	6
6	4	4	8

Question 23. Consider a market with two firms. In the following table, columns labelled as SS_1 and SS_2 give the supply schedules of firm 1 and firm 2 respectively. Compute the market supply schedule.

Price (₹)	0	1	2	3	4	5	6	7	8
SS_1 (kg)	0	0	0	1	2	3	4	5	6
SS_2 (kg)	0	0	0	0	0.5	1	1.5	2	2.5

Answer The Market Supply Schedule

Price (₹)	SS_1 (kg)	SS_2 (kg)	Market Supply $(SS_1 + SS_2)$
0	0	0	0
1	0	0	0
2	0	0	0
3	1	0	1
4	2	0.5	2.5
5	3	1	4
6	4	1.5	5.5
7	5	2	7
8	6	2.5	8.5

Question 24. There are three identical firms in a market. The following table shows the supply schedule of firm 1. Compute the market supply schedule.

Price (₹)	0	1	2	3	4	5	6	7	8
SS_1 (Units)	0	0	2	4	6	8	10	12	14

Answer

Price (₹)	SS_1 (Units)	SS_2 (Units)	SS_3 (Units)	Market Supply $(SS_1+SS_2+SS_3)$
0	0	0	0	0
1	0	0	0	0
2	2	2	2	6
3	4	4	4	12
4	6	6	6	18
5	8	8	8	24
6	10	10	10	30
7	12	12	12	36
8	14	14	14	42

Explanation If the three firms are identical, supply of the each firm will be equal.

Question 25. A firm earns a revenue of ₹ 50 when the market price of a good is ₹ 10. The market price increases to ₹ 15 and the firm now earns a revenue of ₹ 150. What is the price elasticity of the firm's supply curve?

Answer (i) When market price $(P) = 10$

$$\text{Revenue} = ₹\ 50$$

$$\therefore \text{Quantity supplied } (Q) = \frac{50}{10} = 5 \text{ units}$$

(ii) When market price $(P_1) = 15$

$$\text{Revenue} = ₹\ 150$$

$$\therefore \quad \text{Quantity supplied } (Q_1) = \frac{150}{15} = 10 \text{ units}$$

Now given, $\quad P = 10,\ P_1 = 15$

$$Q = 5 \text{ units}$$

$$Q_1 = 10 \text{ units}$$

Change in Price $(\Delta P) = 15 - 10 = ₹\ 5$

Change in Quantity $(\Delta Q) = 10 - 5 = 5$ units

Price elasticity of supply $E_s = \dfrac{\Delta P}{\Delta Q} \times \dfrac{P}{Q}$

$$= \dfrac{5}{5} \times \dfrac{10}{5}$$

$$E_s = 2 \text{ (elastic supply)}$$

Question 26. The market price of a good changes from ₹ 5 to ₹ 20. As a result, the quantity supplied by a firm increases by 15 units. The price elasticity of the firm's supply curve is 0.5. Find the initial and final output levels of the firm.

Answer Given, $P = 5$

New Price $(P_1) = 20$

$$\Delta P = ₹ 15, \Delta Q = 15 \text{ units}$$

Elasticity of supply $(E_s) = 0.5$

Price elasticity of supply $(E_s) = \dfrac{\Delta Q}{\Delta P} \times \dfrac{P}{Q}$

$$0.5 = \dfrac{15}{15} \times \dfrac{5}{Q}$$

Initial Output $(Q) = 10$ units

Final Output $= 10$ units $+ 15$ units $= 25$ units

Question 27. At the market price of ₹ 10, a firm supplies 4 units of output. The market price increases to ₹ 30. The price elasticity of the firm's supply is 1.25. What quantity will the firm supply at the new price?

Answer Given,

$$Q = 4 \text{ units}$$

$$P = ₹ 10, P_1 = ₹ 30$$

Change in price $(\Delta P) = ₹ 20 \ (P - P_1)$

$$E_s = 1.25$$

$$E_s = \dfrac{\Delta Q}{\Delta P} \times \dfrac{P}{Q} = 1.25 = \dfrac{\Delta Q}{20} \times \dfrac{10}{4}$$

$$\Delta Q = 10 \text{ units}$$

$\therefore$ Quantity at new price $= 10 + 4 = 14$ units

5

Market Equilibrium

Points to Remember

1. **Market Equilibrium**   It is a situation of the market in which demand for a commodity is exactly equal to its supply.
2. **Equilibrium Price** Which corresponds to the quantity between market demand and market supply of a commodity.
3. **Equilibrium Quantity** Which corresponds to the equilibrium price in the market.
4. **Excess Demand**   If at any price demand is greater than market supply, it is said excess demand in the market.

$$Y^d > Y^s$$

Here, Y^s = Market Supply

Y^d = Market Demand

5. **Excess Supply**   If at any price market supply is greater than market demand, it is said excess supply in the market.

$$Y^s > Y^d$$

Here, Y^s = Market Supply

Y^d = Market Demand

6. **Non-viable Industry**   The industry for which demand curve and supply do not intersect each other at any positive quantity is called non-viable industry.
7. **Viable Industry**   In case of viable industry supply and demand curve must intersect at same point.

8. **Price Ceiling** Price ceiling means maximum price of a commodity that the seller can charge from the buyers. Often the government fixes this price much below the equilibrium market price of a commodity, so that it becomes within the reach of the poorer sections of the society.

9. **Price Floor** It means the minimum price fixed by the government for a commodity in the market. It seems paradoxical.
   (i) Each firm employs labour up to the point where the marginal revenue product of labour equals the wage rate.
   (ii) With supply curve remaining unchanged when demand curve shifts rightward (leftward), the equilibrium quantity increases (decreases) and equilibrium price increases with fixed number of firms.
   (iii) With demand curve remaining unchanged when supply curve shifts rightward (leftward), the equilibrium quantity increases (decreases) and equilibrium price decrease (increases) with fixed number of firm.

10. **Effect of a Simultaneous Change in Demand and Supply on Equilibrium Price**
   (i) When demand increases more than supply, equilibrium price will increase.
   (ii) When demand and supply increases equally, equilibrium price remain constant.
   (iii) When supply increases more than demand, equilibrium price falls.

QR Code Questions

Question 1. Let us assume, the price of a textbook is ₹ 300. At this price, the publisher is expected to sell 1,000 copies of the textbook. If the price of the textbook is reduced to ₹ 250, then what quantity of textbooks should the publisher sell?

(a) More than 1,000 copies
(b) There will be no change in the sale of textbooks
(c) Its sale will depend on the advertisement policy
(d) Less than 1,000 copies

Answer (a) More than 1,000 copies

Question 2. If a builder is constructing residential flats much faster than the people living in that area or city would like to buy them, then what will be the market condition of these flats?

(a) The builder will continue to build more flats

(b) Supply of flats is more than its demand, so their price will fall

(c) There will be no change in the supply of flats

(d) Supply of flats is more than its demand, so their price will rise

Answer   (b) Supply of flats is more than its demand, so their price will fall

Exercises

Question 1. Explain market equilibrium.

Answer   Market Equilibrium is a situation where the quantity demanded becomes equal to quantity supplied, corresponding to a particular price.

It means $\Rightarrow$ Market demand = Market supply

Question 2. When do we say there is excess demand for a commodity in the market?

Answer When the market demand exceeds market supply of a commodity at a given price then there is an excess demand for a commodity in the market.

Question 3. When do we say that there is excess supply for a commodity in the market?

Answer   When the market supply of a commodity is greater than market demand, at a given price then there is an excess supply for a commodity in the market.

Question 4. What will happen if the price prevailing in the market is

(i) above the equilibrium price?

(ii) below the equilibrium price?

Answer

(i) If the price prevailing in the market is above equilibrium price, demand will be less than supply. It means a situation of excess supply in the market.

(ii) If the price prevailing in the market is below the equilibrium price, demand will be more than supply. It means a situation of excess demand.

Question 5. Explain how price is determined in a perfectly competitive market with fixed number of firms.

Answer   Equilibrium price is determined by the market forces of demand and supply in a perfectly competitive market. Where market equilibrium is determined when market demand is equal to market supply, under perfect competition.

Market demand is the sum total of demand for a commodity by all the

(i) buyers in the market. Its curve slopes downward due to law of demand.

(ii) Market supply is the sum total of supplies of a commodity by all the firms in the market. Its curve slopes upwards due to law of supply.

Considering market demand schedule on the one hand and market supply schedule on the other, indentify equilibrium price on the one where Market demand = Market supply. It means market demand curve and market supply curve intersect each other.

Explanation by Table and Figure

Price of Commodity (₹)	Market Demand (Units)	Market Supply (Units)	
5	100	20	Equilibrium level (Demand = Supply)
7	80	40	
9	60	60	
11	40	80	
15	20	100	

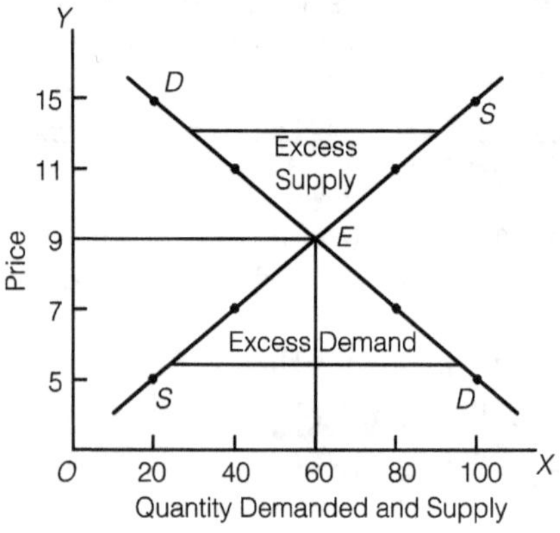

Note *Market equilibrium is determined at point E, where price ₹ 9. So, equilibrium price is determined at ₹ 9.*

Question 6. Suppose the price at which equilibrium is attained in exercise 5 is above the minimum average cost of the firms constituting the market. Now, if we allow for free entry and exit of firms, how will the market price adjust to it?

Answer   The equilibrium price is ₹ 9 in the above figure of Q-5 which is above the minimum of average cost. It implies that firm is earning supernormal profit. This situation attracts new firms, the industry supply of output also increases. New firms will continue to enter the industry which leads the price to fall until it becomes equal to minimum average cost.At this stage firms starts earning normal profit.

Question 7. At what level of price do the firms in a perfectly competitive market supply when free entry and exit is allowed in the market? How is equilibrium quantity determined in such a market?

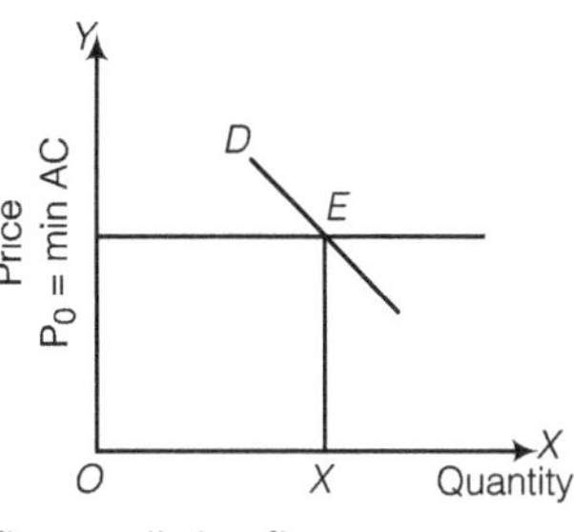

Answer Equilibrium price will always be equal to minimum average cost in the long run as due to the free entry and exit of the firms, all the firms earn zero economic profit.

Question 8. How is the equilibrium number of firms determined in a market where entry and exit is permitted?

Answer With the free entry and exit, the equilibrium number of firms determined in a market by equilibrium quantity supply per firm.

or   Equilibrium number of firms $= \dfrac{\text{Equilibrium quantity}}{\text{Supply of each firm}}$

Question 9. How are equilibrium price and quantity affected when income of the consumers

    (i) increase?   (ii) decrease?

Answer

    (i) When income of the consumers increase then demand will also increase. But it is possible only in case of normal goods. As result there is an increase in both equilibrium price and equilibrium quantity.

    Diagram (i)

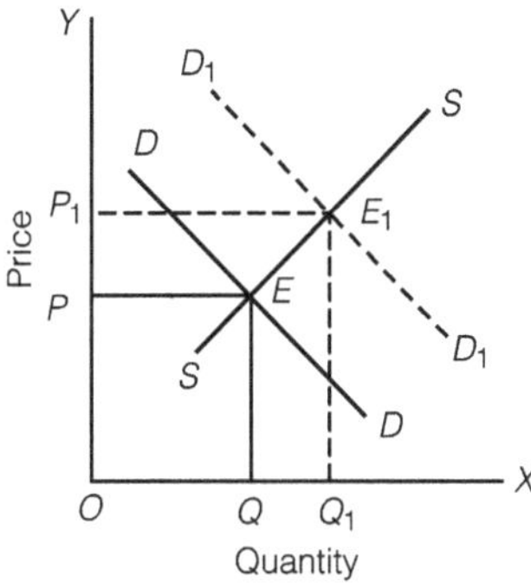

    (ii) When income of consumer decrease, then demand will also decrease (in case of normal goods only). As a result demand curve shifts leftward and both equilibrium price and quantity will decrease.

Diagram (ii)

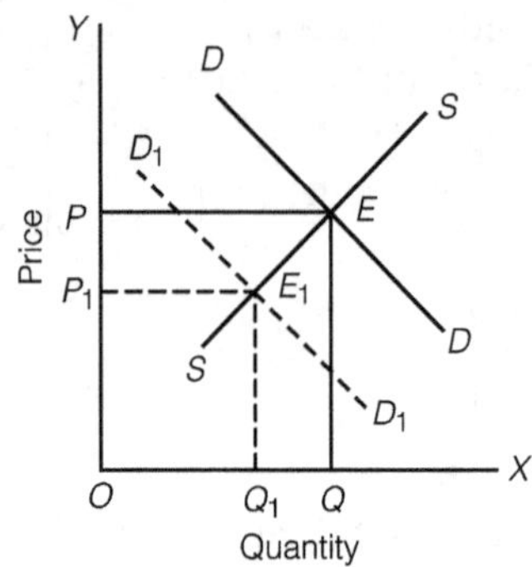

Question 10. Using supply and demand curves, show how an increase in the price of shoes affects the price of a pair of socks and the number of pairs of socks bought and sold.

Answer Shoes and socks are complementary goods. An increase in the price of shoes will cause a decrease in demand of socks. It will lead to excess supply. This leads to competition among sellers, which reduces the price. Fall in price leads to decrease in supply and rise in demand. These changes continue till supply and demand become equal at a new equilibrium price. As a result there is a decrease in demand of both shoes and socks.

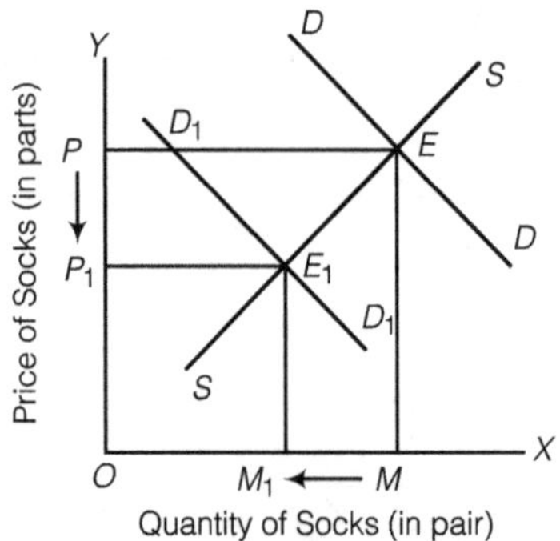

Question 11. How will a change in price of coffee affect the equilibrium price of tea? Explain the effect on equilibrium quantity also through a diagram.

Answer Tea and coffee are substitute goods. A change in price of coffee will directly influence the equilibrium price and quantity of tea . As a result, the demand curve of tea will shift to the right (in case of an increase in the price of coffee).

The supply curve of tea remain same this will lead to an increase in price of tea (P_1) and increase in quantity (X_1).

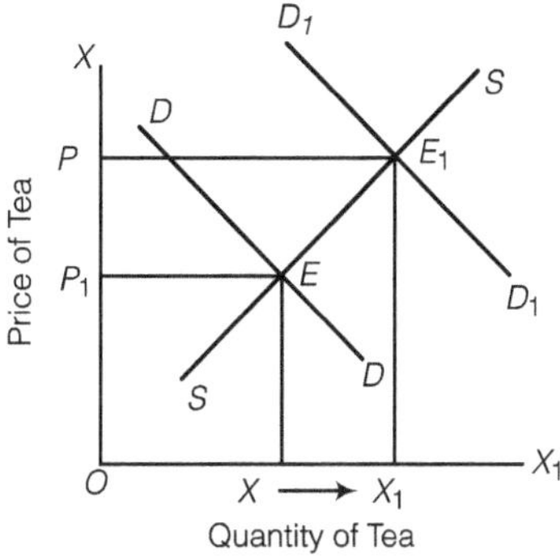

Question 12. How do the equilibrium price and quantity of a commodity change when price of input used in its production changes?

Answer   A change in price of inputs will directly affect the equilibrium price and quantity of goods.

An increase in the price of an input, increase the unit cost of production of the commodity. This will cause a decrease in the supply of a commodity and leads to a leftward shift of supply curve. But the demand curve will remain the same because market price of commodity will rise and quantity will fall.

As a result supply will decrease and supply curve shift leftward as in figure

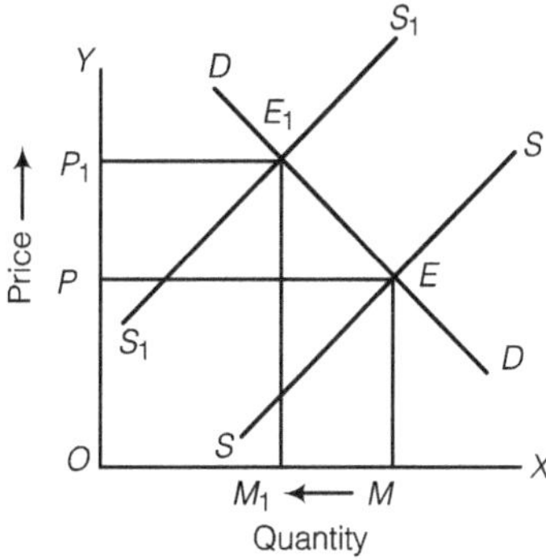

Question 13. If the price of a substitute (y) of goods (x) increases, what impact does it have on the equilibrium price and quantity of good x?

Answer An increase in price of a substitute (y) of goods (x) will directly affect the equilibrium price and quantity of goods (x). Rise in price of (y) will relatively cheaper and demand for (x) will rise. It will lead to excess demand. It will lead to increase in both equilibrium price and equilibrium quantity.

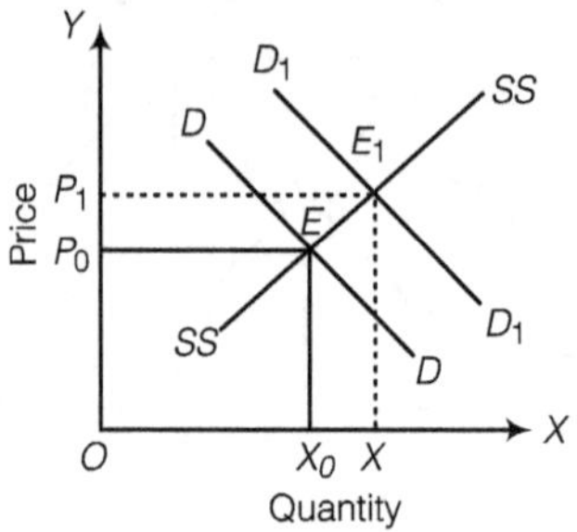

Question 14. Compare the effect of shift in demand curve on the equilibrium when the number of firms in the market is fixed with the situation when entry-exit is permitted.

Answer If demand increase, then it creates excess demand for the goods. It will lead to increase in price and in supernormal profit. This will attract entry of new firms, and it will lead to minimum AC.

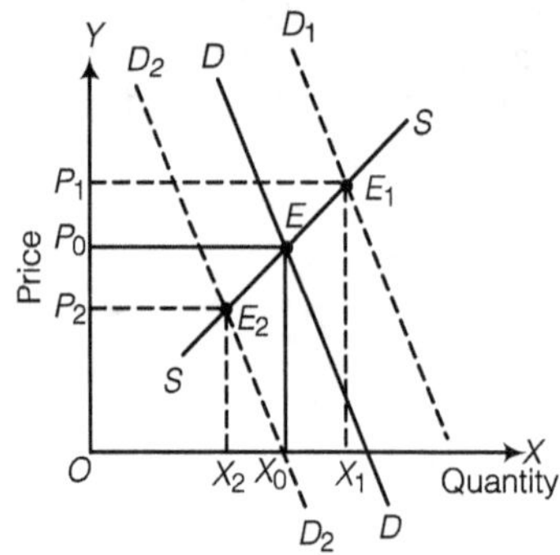

The effect of shift in demand curve when number of firms in the market is fixed.

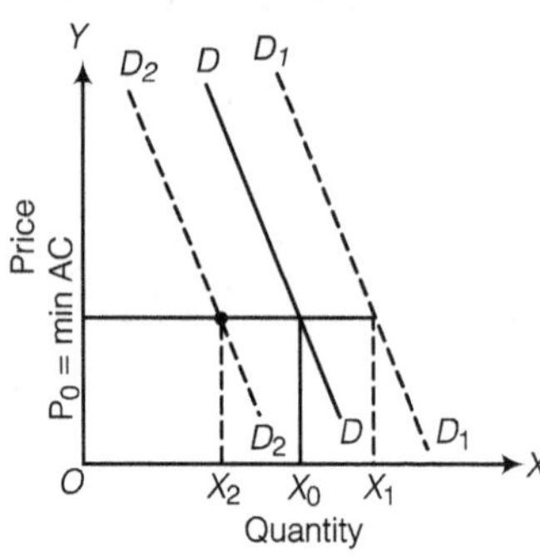

The effect of shift in demand curve when entry and exit remitted.

Question 15. Explain through a diagram the effect of a rightward shift of both the demand and supply curves on equilibrium price and quantity.

Answer As a result equilibrium price remains unchanged.

When both demand and supply of a commodity increase, the equilibrium quantity will increase but equilibrium price may or may not be affected.

There may be following three situations

(i) The equilibrium price will remain the same, if demand and supply of a commodity increase in equal ratio.

Diagram as

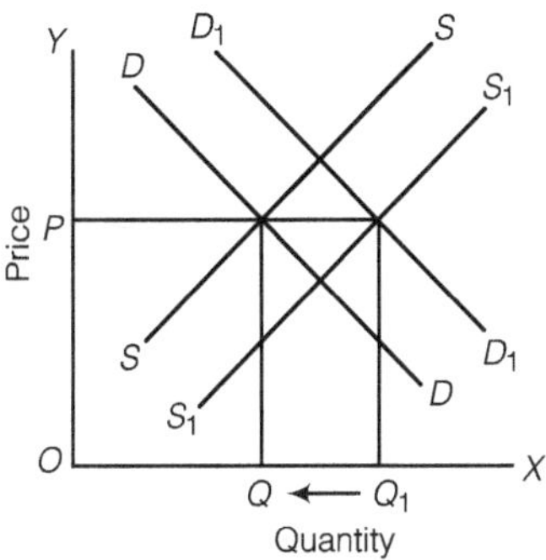

(ii) Equilibrium price will rise, if both demand and supply increase but increase in demand is more than the increase in supply.

Diagram as

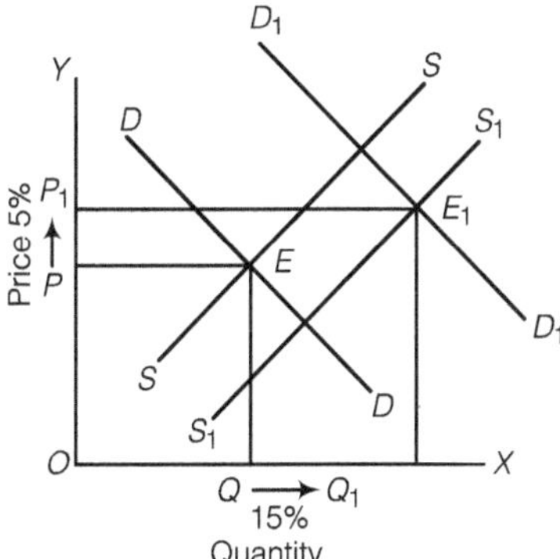

(iii) Equilibrium price will fall, if both demand and supply increase but the increase in demand is less than increase in supply.

Diagram as

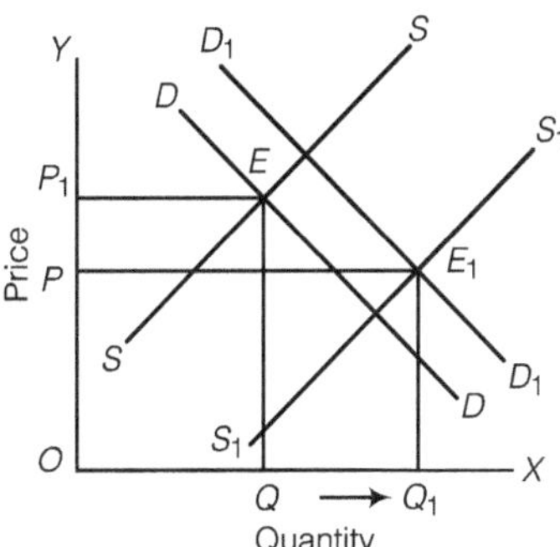

Question 16. How are the equilibrium price and quantity affected when

    (a) both demand and supply curves shift in the same directions?

    (b) demand and supply curves shift in opposite directions?

Answer

    (a) When both demand and supply curves shift in same direction (shift to left) the equilibrium quantity will fall but equilibrium price may or may not be affected.

    There may be three situations

    (i) Equilibrium price will go up, when decrease in demand is less than decrease in supply.

Diagram (i)

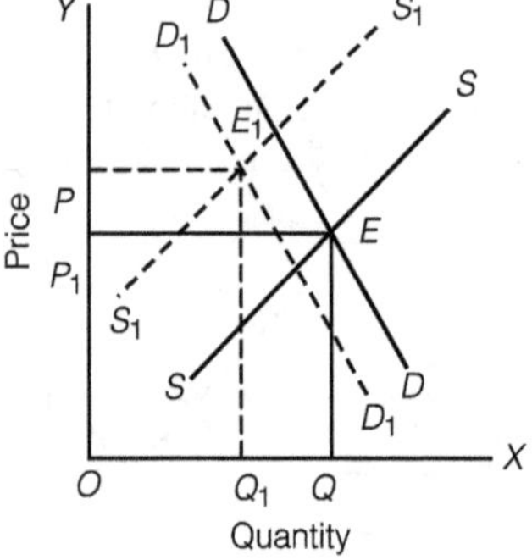

    (ii) Equilibrium price will fall, when decrease in demand is more than decrease in supply.

Diagram (ii)

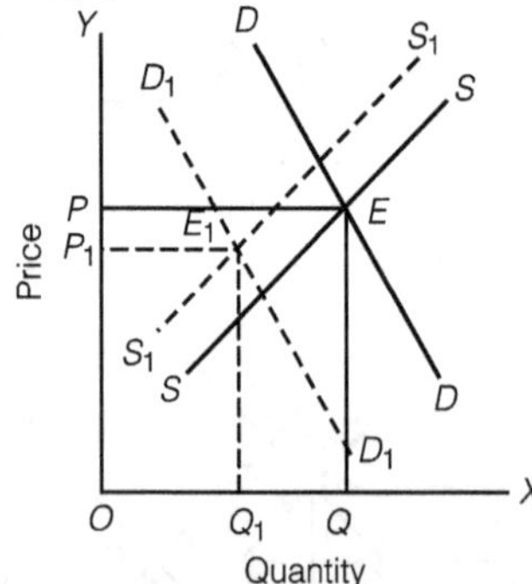

    (iii) No change in equilibrium price, when decrease in demand is equal to decrease in supply.

Diagram (iii)

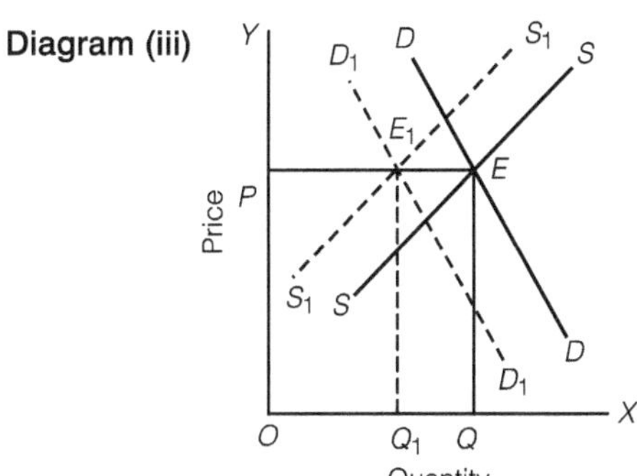

(b) When demand and supply curves shift in opposite directions (demand curve shift to left and supply curve to the right), the equilibrium price will fall but the equilibrium quantity may or may not be affected. There may be three situations

(i) The equilibrium quantity will rise, when decrease in demand is less than increase in supply.

Diagram (i)

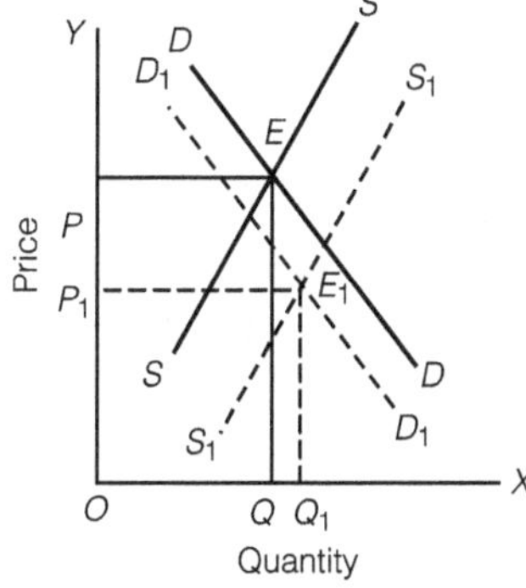

(ii) The equilibrium quantity will fall, when decrease in demand is more than increase in supply.

Diagram (ii)

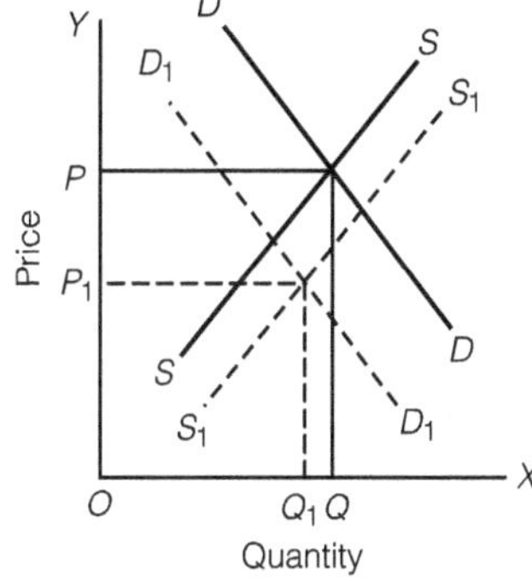

(iii) No change in equilibrium quantity, when decrease in demand is equal to the increase in supply.

Diagram (iii)

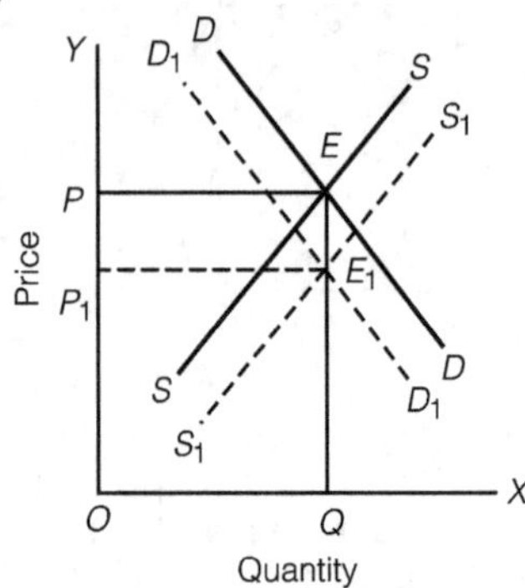

Question 17. In what respect do the supply and demand curves in the labour market differ from those in the goods market?

Answer

(i) Supply of labour is provided by households whereas demand for commodities is from the households.

(ii) The supply of commodities is by the firms, whereas demand for labour is by the firms.

Question 18. How is the optimal amount of labour determined in a perfectly competitive market?

Answer The optimal amount of labour determined in a perfectly competitive market as

$$VMP_L = W$$

where W = Wage rate

VMP_L = Value of Marginal Product of Labour

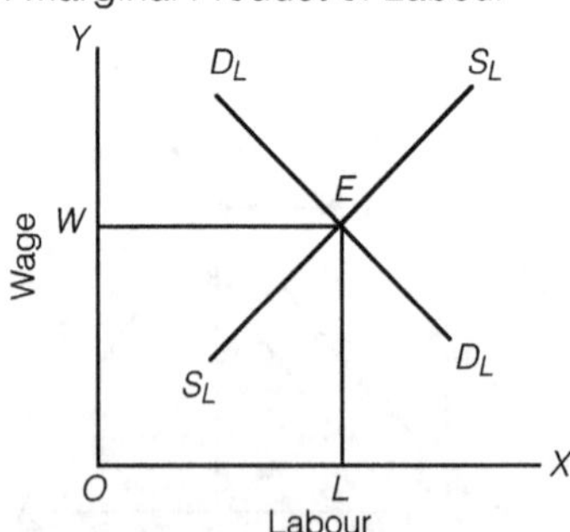

Here $D_L = S_L$ (Demand and Supply of labour) thus the OL is the optimal amount of labour at Equilibrium point E.

Question 19. How is the wage rate determined in a perfectly competitive labour market?

Answer The wage rate determined in a perfectly competitive labour market by the intersection of demand and supply of labour.

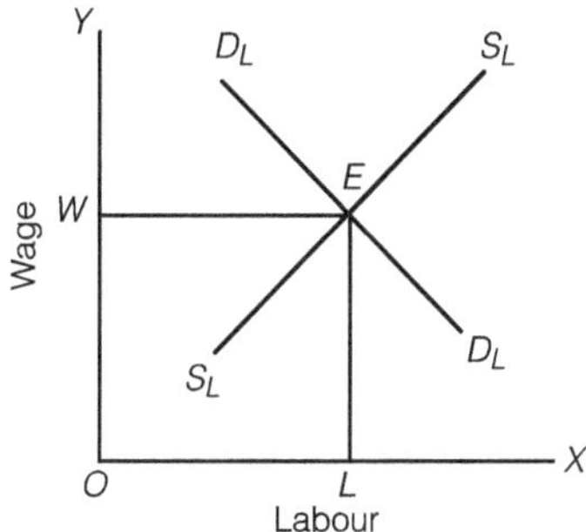

$D_L = S_L$, it occurs equilibrium at point E. It define equilibrium wage and optimal amount of labour. Therefore, OW is the wage rate in a perfectly competitive market.

Question 20. Can you think of any commodity on which price ceiling is imposed in India? What may be the consequences of price ceiling?

Answer Price ceiling means the maximum price. In this condition the market price below the equilibrium price consequences of price ceiling are

  (i) Excess demand

  (ii) Emergence of black market

  (iii) Rationing due to shortage of supply of the commodity

Question 21. A shift in demand curve has a larger effect on price and smaller effect on quantity when the number of firms is fixed compared to the situation when free entry and exit is permitted. Explain.

Answer Under the long run, when free entry and exit is permitted, there is total changes in quantity but no change in equilibrium price. It happens when the demand curve intersects the supply curve at equilibrium point, then Price =minimum Average cost. As a result demand curve shift upward, it effect, there is no change in price but quantity rises.

When the number of firms is fixed, the supply curve is upward and demand curve is downward sloping. It results the demand effect more in price than quantity.

Question 22. Suppose the demand and supply curve of commodity X in a perfectly competitive market are given by

$$q_D = 700 - p$$
$$q_S = 500 + 3p \text{ for } p \geq 15$$
$$= 0 \text{ for } 0 \leq p < 15$$

Assume that the market consists of identical firms. Identify the reason behind the market supply of commodity X being zero at any price less than ₹ 15. What will be the equilibrium price for this commodity? At equilibrium, what quantity of X will be produced?

Answer From the given supply curve, it can be concluded that ₹ 15 must be the minimum Average Variable Cost (AVG) of producing commodity X. In a perfectly competitive market, firms do not produce positive level of output for any price less than AVG as they will be at loss, if they supply at a price less than AVC. Thus, firms will not produce commodity X at any price less than ₹ 15.

Calculation of Equilibrium Price and Equilibrium Quantity

At equilibrium, $q_D = q_S$

So,　　　　　　　　　　　　$700 - p = 500 + 3p$

$\Rightarrow$　　　　　　　　　　　　$4p = 200$

Thus, Equilibrium Price(p) = ₹ 50.

Putting the value of equilibrium price in the equation of demand curve

Equilibrium Quantity $(q_D) = 700 - 50 = 650$ units.

Question 23. Considering the same demand curve as in exercise 22, now let us allow for free entry and exit of the firms producing commodity X. Also assume the market consists of identical firms producing commodity X. Let the supply curve of a single firm be explained as

$$q_f^s = 8 + 3p \text{ for } p \geq 20 = 0 \text{ for } 0 \leq p < 20$$

(a) What is the significance of p = 20?

(b) At what price will the market for X be in equilibrium? State the reason for your answer.

(c) Calculate the equilibrium quantity and number of firms.

Answer $q_f^s = 8 + 3p$ for $p \geq$ ₹ 200 $= 0$ for $0 \leq p <$ ₹ 20

$$q_d = 700 - p$$

(a) For the price between 0 to 20, no firm is going to produce anything as the price in this range is below the minimum of LAC. So, at the price of ₹ 20, the price line is equal to the minimum of LAC.

(b) As there exists the freedom of entry and exit of firms, the minimum of AVC is at ₹ 20, also, the price of ₹ 20 is the equilibrium price. This is because in the long run, all firms earn zero economic profit, which implies that the price of ₹ 20 is the equilibrium price and at any price lower than ₹ 20, the firm will move out of the market.

(c) At equilibrium price of ₹ 20

Quantity supplied $= q_s = 8 + 3p = 8 + 3(20)$

$$\Rightarrow \qquad q_s = 68 \text{ units}$$

Quantity demanded $q_d = 700 - p = 700 - 20$

$$\Rightarrow \qquad q_d = 680$$

Number of firms $(n) = \dfrac{q_d}{q_s}$

$$n = \dfrac{680}{68}$$

$$n = 10 \text{ firms}$$

Therefore, the number of firms in the market is 10 and the equilibrium quantity in 680 units.

Question 24. Suppose the demand and supply curves of salt are given by

$$q_D = 1{,}000 - p; \; q_S = 700 + 2p$$

(a) Find the equilibrium price and quantity.

(b) Now suppose that the price of an input used to produce salt has increased so that the new supply curve is $q_S = 400 + 2p$

How does the equilibrium price and quantity change? Does the change conform to your expectation?

(c) Suppose the government has imposed a tax of ₹ 3 per unit of sale of salt. How does it affect the equilibrium price and quantity?

Answer

(a) At equilibrium price, $Q_d = Q_s$

$\therefore 1{,}000 - p = 700 + 2p \Rightarrow 3p = 300 \Rightarrow p = 100$

Now, putting the value of equilibrium price into the demand curve equation, we get

$$Q_d = 1{,}000 - p = 1{,}000 - 100 = 900$$

So, equilibrium quantity is 900 units.

(b) If the price of input used increases, then the new supply curve becomes

$$Q_s = 400 + 2p$$

For equilibrium, $Q_d = Q_s$

$\therefore$ $1{,}000 - p = 400 + 2p$

$\Rightarrow$ $3p = 600 \Rightarrow p = 200$

So, equilibrium price = ₹ 200

Substituting p = 200 into demand equation, we get

Equilibrium quantity $= 1{,}000 - p = 1{,}000 - 200 = 800$

So, equilibrium price increases and equilibrium quantity falls due to rise in the price of inputs.

(c) If tax of ₹ 3 per unit of sale is imposed on the commodity, then the new supply curve becomes

$Q_s = 700 + 2(p - 3)$

$\Rightarrow$ $Q_s = 700 + 2p - 6 \Rightarrow Q_s = 694 + 2p$

For equilibrium, $Q_d = Q_s$

$$1{,}000 - p = 694 + 2p$$
$$1{,}000 - 694 = 3p$$

$\Rightarrow$ $3p = 306 \Rightarrow p = 102$

So, equilibrium price = ₹ 102

Substituting $p = 102$ to demand equation, we get

Equilibrium quantity $= 1{,}000 - 102 = 898$

Thus, the equilibrium price increases and equilibrium quantity decreases.

Question 25. Suppose the market determined rent for apartments is too high for common people to afford. If the government comes forward to help those seeking arguments on rent by imposing control on rent, what impact will it have on the market for apartments?

Answer If the government imposes price ceiling by Rent Control Act (the maximum price) that can be charged as the rent of apartment. It results decline in equilibrium price due to

(i) excess demand of apartments.
(ii) black marketing by builders.

6

Non-Competitive Markets

Points to Remember

1. **Market** It refers to a mechanism or an arrangement that facilitates contact between the buyers and sellers for the sale and purchase of goods and services.

2. **Monopoly** It is a form of the market in which there is a single seller of a product with no close substitutes.

   Example- Railways in India are a monopoly industry of the Government of India.

3. **Features of Monopoly**
   (i) One seller and large number of buyers
   (ii) Restrictions the entry of new firms
   (iii) No, close substitutes   (iv) Full control over price
   (v) Price discrimination

4. **Price Maker** A monopolist is a price maker. It means that he can fix whatever price he wishes to fix for his product.

5. **How does a Monopoly Market Structure Arise?**
   (i) Government licensing   (ii) Patent rights
   (iii) Cartels   (iv) Natural occurrence

6. **Monopolistic Competition** It is a form of the market in which there are many sellers of the product but the product of each seller is some what different from that of the other.

7. **Features of Monopolistic Competition**
   (i) Large number of buyers and sellers
   (ii) Product differentiation

   (iii) Freedom of entry and exit of firm
   (iv) Selling cost   (v) Less mobility
   (vi) Lack of perfect knowledge
   (vii) Non-price competition (viii) More can be sold at lower price

8. **Oligopoly** It is a form of the market in which there are a few big sellers of a commodity and a large number of buyers. Each seller has a significant share of the market.

9. **Features of Oligopoly**
   (i) A few firms   (ii) Large number of buyer
   (iii) Entry barriers
   (iv) High degree of interdependence
   (v) Not possible to determine firm's demand curve
   (vi) Formation of cartels   (vii) Non-price competition

10. Firm's demand curve is indeterminate under oligopoly because there is a high degree of interdependence between the firm.

11. Shape of demand curve under different market
   (i) It slops downwards under monopoly. But it is not very elastic.
   (ii) It slops downwards under monopolistic competition. But it is relatively more elastic.
   (iii) It is indeterminate under oligopoly.

QR Code Questions

Question 1. There is an inverse relation between price and demand for

   (a) monopolistic competition
   (b) perfect competition only
   (c) both monopoly and monopolistic competition
   (d) monopoly only

Answer   (c) both monopoly and monopolistic competition

Question 2.

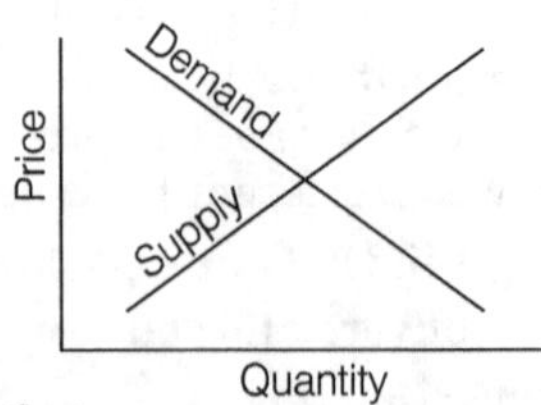

Law of demand states that

(a) other things remaining the same, with the increase in price quantity decreases

(b) quantity does not change with any increase in price

(c) with the increase in price, quantity increases

(d) with the decrease in quantity price also decreases

Answer   (a) other things remaining the same, with the increase in price quantity decreases

This concept is explained in Chapter-2 (Part A) of NCERT Book.

Question 3. In monopoly there is/are

(a) single seller, large number of buyers

(b) large corporation

(c) large number of sellers and buyers

(d) many firms

Answer   (a) single seller, large number of buyers

Question 4.

In duopoly, there is/are

(a) Two firms controlling the market

(b) Large corporation

(c) Only one firm   (d) Many firms

Answer   (a) Two firms controlling the market

Question 5. What microeconomics is about?

(a) Study of financial position of the economy

(b) Study of the economy at macro level

(c) Study of the economy at micro level

(d) Study of business environment

Answer   (c) Study of the economy at micro level

This concept is explained in Chapter-1 (Part-A) of NCERT Book.

Question 6. Which of the following statements is appropriate for monopoly?

    (a) Both AR and MR curve are downward sloping and MR is below AR curve.

    (b) AR curve is downward sloping whereas, MR is upward sloping.

    (c) Both AR and MR curve are downward sloping and AR is below MR curve.

    (d) MR is constant but AR is rising.

Answer (a) Both AR and MR curve are downward sloping and MR is below AR curve.

Question 7.

How is AR and MR curves represented in the case of perfect competition?

    (a) Vertical straight line

    (b) Both AR and MR curves slope downward

    (c) Right angled

    (d) Horizontal straight line

Answer (d) Horizontal straight line

Question 8. When prices are constant, then average revenue is greater than marginal revenue?

    (a) True   (b) False

Answer (b) False. When price is constant, AR is also constant. Thus, when price is constant, AR=MR.

This concept is explained in Chapter-4 (Part-A) of NCERT Book.

Exercises

Question 1. What would be shape of demand curve, so that the total revenue curve is

(i) A positively sloped straight line passing through the origin?

(ii) A horizontal line?

Answer

(i) Demand curve or AR curve will be a horizontal straight parallel to the X-axis because positively sloped straight line TR curve passing through the origin indicates that price remains constant at all level of output .

(ii) Demand curve will slope downwards from left to right because horizontal TR indicates that TR remains same at levels of output. It is possible only when price falls with rise in output.

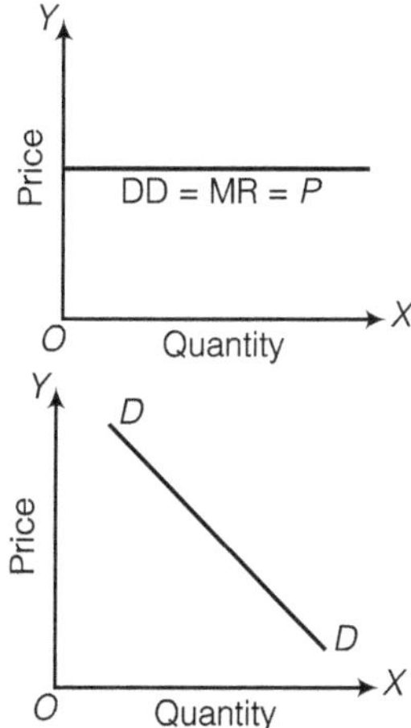

Question 2. From the schedule provided below calculate the total revenue, demand curve and the price elasticity of demand.

Q	1	2	3	4	5	6	7	8	9
MR	10	6	2	2	2	0	0	0	-5

Answer

Quantity (Q)	Marginal Revenue (MR)	Total Revenue (TR)	Demand Curve (AR) = TR/Q	Price Elasticity of Demand $e_d = \dfrac{\Delta Q}{\Delta P} \times \dfrac{P}{Q}$
1	10	10	10	
2	6	16	8	$e_d = 5$
3	2	18	6	2 $\quad$ $e > 1$
4	2	20	5	2
5	2	22	4.5	2.5
6	0	22	3.6	1 $\quad$ $e = 1$
7	0	22	3.1	1.2
8	0	22	2.7	1.1
9	-5	17	1.9	0.38 $\quad$ $e < 1$

Question 3. What is the value of the MR when the demand curve is elastic?

Answer When the demand curve is elastic, then MR will be positive. It means $e > 1$ and $MR = p\left(1 - \dfrac{1}{e_d}\right)$

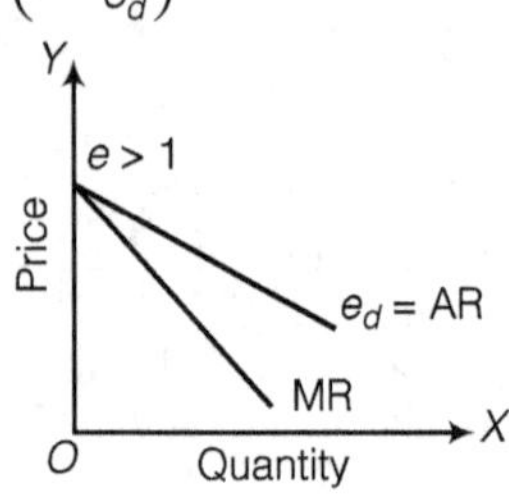

Question 4. A monopoly firm has a total fixed cost of ₹100 and has the following demand schedule

Quantity	1	2	3	4	5	6	7	8	9	10
Price	100	90	80	70	60	50	40	30	20	10

Find the short-run equilibrium quantity, price and total profit. What would be the equilibrium in the long-run? In case the total cost was ₹ 1,000, describe the equilibrium in the short-run and in the long-run.

Answer

Quantity (Q)	Price	TR $= P \times Q$
1	100	100
2	90	180
3	80	240
4	70	280
5	60	300
6	50	300
7	40	280
8	30	240
9	20	180
10	10	100

The total cost of the monopolist firm is zero, the profit will be maximum where TR is maximum. As, in the above case, TR is maximum at the 6th unit of output.

Profit of the firm = 300

Short-run equilibrium price = ₹ 50

Profit = TR – TC = 300 – 0 = 300

As per the case if the total cost is ₹ 1,000 then

$$= 300 - 1,000 = -700$$

∴ The firm is earning loss in the short-run and it hill stop its production in the long-run.

Question 5. If the monopolist firm of exercise 3, was a public sector firm. The government set a rule for its manager to accept the government fixed price as given (*i.e.*, to be a price taker and therefore behave as a firm in a perfectly competitive market) and the government decide to set the price so that demand and supply in the market are equal. What would be the equilibrium price, quantity and profit in that case?

Answer Equilibrium price = P_1

Equilibrium quantity = Q_1

Profit = Normal profit

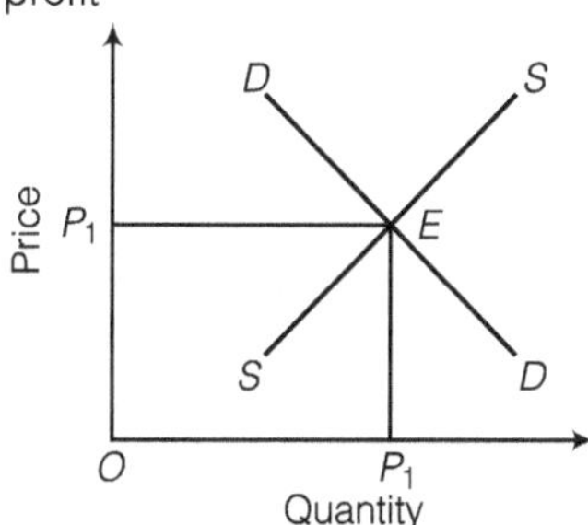

In a perfectly competitive market a firm earns zero profit. It implies that a competitive firm can get only normal profit.

Question 6. Comment on the shape of MR curve in case the TR curve is a

(i) Positively sloped straight line.

(ii) Horizontal straight line.

Answer

(i) When TR curve is positively sloped straight line, MR curve will be a horizontal like parallel to the X-axis. It shows AR and MR is constant at each level of output.

(ii) When TR curve is a horizontal line, then MR will be zero because horizontal TR indicates that it remains constant at levels of output.

Question 7. The market demand curve for a commodity and the total cost for a monopoly firm producing the commodity is given by the schedules below. Use the information to calculate the following

Quantity	0	1	2	3	4	5	6	7	8
Price	52	44	37	31	26	22	19	16	13
Total Cost	10	60	90	100	102	105	109	115	125

(i) The MR and MC schedules.

(ii) The quantities for which the MR and MC are equal.

(iii) The equilibrium quantity of output and the equilibrium price of the commodity.

(iv) The total revenue, total cost and total profit in equilibrium.

Answer (i)   **MR Schedules**

Q	P	$TR = P \times Q$	MR
0	52	0	—
1	44	44	44
2	37	74	30
3	31	93	19
4	26	104	11
5	22	110	6
6	19	114	4
7	16	112	−2
8	13	104	−8

MC Schedules

Q	TC	MC
0	10	—
1	60	50
2	90	40
3	100	10
4	102	2
5	105	3
6	109	4
7	115	6
8	125	10

(ii) MR = MC at 6th unit of output

(iii) Equilibrium quantity = 6 units

       Equilibrium price = ₹ 19

(iv) At equilibrium point

Total revenue $= 114$

Total cost $= 109$

Total profit $= 114 - 109 = ₹ 5$

Question 8. Will the monopolist firm continue to produce in the short-run if a loss is incurred at the best short-run level of output?

Answer In the the short-run of a firm incurrs loss the continuation to produce determined given below.

(i) If a this level of output MC curve cuts the MR curve from above or MC curve is negatively sloped then the firm will continue to produce in the short-run if a loss is incurred. Beyond this level of output firm may earn profit as MC is sloping downward.

(ii) If at this level of output MC curve cuts the MR curve from below or MC curve is rising then the firm will not continue to produce in the short-run if a loss is incurred.

Question 9. Explain why the demand curve facing a firm under monopolistic competition is negatively sloped.

Answer Demand of the product is not in the central of monopoly firm because it has no close substitutes. In order to increase the output to be sold, monopolist will have to reduce the price. Therefore, monopoly firm faces a downward sloping demand curve.

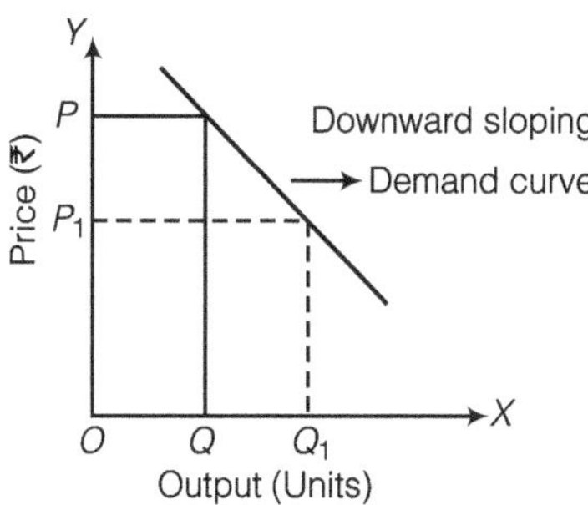

In figure, at price OP, firm can sell OQ quantity. Demand rises to OQ_1 if the price is reduced to OP.

So, demand curve under monopoly is negatively sloped as more quantity can be sold only at a lower price.

Question 10. What is the reason for the long-run equilibrium of a firm in monopolistic competition to be associated with zero profit?

Answer   In monopolistic competition the number of firms is large. There is free entry and exit of firms. The goods produced are differenciated. In the short-run a firm may earn abnormal profit which attracts the new firms. It will expand the output of the commodity. It will cause fall in the market price of the commodity. This phenomenon of entry of firms, expansion of output and falling of price will continue till profit become zero. At this level of profit there will be no attraction for new firms to enter in the market.

Contrary to it if firms are facing losses in the short-run. Some firms would stop producing the commodity. It results in contraction of output that will dead to a higher price. The exit would half once profits become zero.

Thus, entry or exit of firms in long-run half once profits become zero and this would serve as the long-run equilibrium.

Question 11. List the three different ways in which oligopoly firms may behave.

Answer   Following are the three different ways in which oligopoly firm may behave.

(i) Duopoly firms may collude together and decide not to compete with each other and maximise total profits.

(ii) Each of the two firms decide how much quantity to produce and would not change the quantity that is supplying.

(iii) In oligopoly the market price does not move freely in response to changes in demand.

Question 12. If duopoly behaviour is one that is described by Cournot, the market demand curve is given by the equation $q = 200 - 4p$ and both the firms have zero costs, firms the quantity supplied by each firm in equilibrium and the equilibrium market price.

Answer   Market demand curve

$$Q = 200 - 4p$$

When the demand curve is a straight line and total cost is zero

At $P = ₹\,0$, market demand is

$$Q = 200 - 4\,(0) = 200 \text{ units}$$

If firm B does not produce anything, then the market demand faced by firm A is 200 units.

$\therefore$ The supply of firm $A = \dfrac{1}{2} \times 200 = 100$ units

In the next round, the portion of market demand faced by firm B is

$$200 - \frac{200}{2} = 200 - 100 = 100 \text{ units}$$

$\therefore$ Firm B would supply $\frac{1}{2} \times \left(200 - \frac{200}{2}\right) = 50$ units

Thus, firm B has changed its supply from zero to 50 units. To this firm A would react accordingly and the demand faced by firm A will be

$$200 - \frac{1}{2} \times \left(200 - \frac{200}{2}\right) = 200 - 50 = 150 \text{ units}$$

$\therefore$ Firm A would supply $= \frac{150}{2} = 75$ units

The quantity supplied by firm A and firm B is represented in the table below.

Round	Firm	Quantity Supplied
1.	B	0
2.	A	$\frac{1}{2} \times 200 = \frac{200}{2} = 100$
3.	B	$\frac{1}{2}\left[200 - \frac{1}{2} \times 200\right] = \frac{200}{2} - \frac{200}{4}$
4.	A	$\frac{1}{2}\left[200 - \frac{1}{2}\left(200 - \frac{1}{2} \times 200\right)\right] = \frac{200}{2} - \frac{200}{4} + \frac{200}{8}$
5.	B	$\frac{1}{2}\left\{200 - \frac{1}{2}\left[200 - \frac{1}{2}\left(200 - \frac{1}{2} \times 200\right)\right]\right\} = \frac{200}{2} - \frac{200}{4} + \frac{200}{8} - \frac{200}{16}$

Therefore, the equilibrium output supplied by firm A

$$= \frac{200}{2} - \frac{200}{4} + \frac{200}{8} - \frac{200}{16} + \frac{200}{32} - \frac{200}{64} + \frac{200}{128} - \frac{200}{256} + \ldots = \frac{200}{3} \text{ units}$$

Similarly, the equilibrium output supplied by firm $B = \frac{200}{3}$ units.

Market supply = Supply by firm A + Supply by firm B

$$= \frac{200}{3} + \frac{200}{3}$$

Equilibrium output or market supply $= Q = \frac{400}{3}$ units — (1)

For Equilibrium Price

$$Q = 200 - 4p$$
$$4p = 200 - Q$$
$$p = 50 - \frac{Q}{4}$$

$$p = 50 - \frac{1}{4}\left(\frac{400}{3}\right)$$

$$p = 50 - \frac{100}{3}$$

$$p = \frac{150 - 100}{3}$$

$$p = ₹\frac{50}{3}$$

$$\therefore \quad \text{Equilibrium output} = \frac{400}{3}$$

$$\text{Equilibrium price} = \frac{50}{3}$$

Question 13. What is meant by prices being rigid? How can oligopoly behaviour lead to such an outcome?

Answer Price rigidity means price under oligopoly tends to be fixed or constant despite the changes in demand and cost in the industry.

The oligopoly firms react to a change in price initiated by any firm. The firm believes that its rivals will react after the analysis of what the changes made by oligopoly firm.

The firm believes that if it raises the price the rivals will not follow it but if the firms cuts down the price the rival firms will also do the same. Thus, in oligopoly firm prefers to stick at the existing price.

PART-B

Introductory Macroeconomics

1

Introduction

Points to Remember

1. **Macroeconomics** It deals with the aggregate economic variables of an economy.

2. **Capitalist Country** In a capitalist country production activity are mainly carried out by capitalist enterprises.

3. **Wage Rate** There is sale and purchase of labour services at a price which is called the wage rate.

4. **Wage Labour** The labour which is sold and purchased against wages is referred to as wage labour.

5. **Great Depression** Great depression of 1929 and the subsequent year saw the output and employment levels in the countries of the world as well.

6. **Entrepreneurs** People who exercise control over major decisions and bear a large part of the risk associated with the firm/enterprise.

7. **Revenue** The money that is earned is called revenue.

8. **Investment Expenditure** Expenses which raise productive capacity are called Investment Expenditure.

QR Code Questions

Question 1. Depreciation is equal to

    (a) Gross National Product – Personal Income

    (b) Personal Income – Personal Taxes

    (c) Gross National Product – Net National Product

Answer (c) Gross National Product – Net National Product

      This concept is explained in Chapter-2 (Part-B) of NCERT Book.

Question 2. In which market form, a firm is a price maker?

    (a) Monopoly   (b) Duopoly

    (c) Oligopoly   (d) Monopolistic competition

Answer (a) Monopoly

      This concept is explained in Chapter-6 (Part-A) of NCERT Book.

Exercises

Question 1. What is the difference between Microeconomics and Macroeconomics?

Answer Difference between Microeconomics and Macroeconomics

S.No.	Microeconomics	Macroeconomics
1.	Microeconomics studies economic problems at an individual level.	Macroeconomics studies economic problems at the level of an economy as a whole.
2.	Microeconomics is determined the output and price for an individual firms.	Macroeconomics is determined an aggregate output and general price level in the whole economy.
3.	Demand and supply are its main tools.	Aggregate demand and aggregate supply are its main tools.
4.	It assumes all the macro variables to be constant as national income, consumption, saving etc.	It assumes that all the micro variables to be constant as households, firms, prices of Individual product etc.

Question 2. What are the important features of a capitalist economy?

Answer Features of capitalist economy are

1. It is an economic system in which no restriction is imposed by government and every individual is enjoying economic freedom.

2. Factors of production are privately owned.

3. Profit maximisation is prime consideration.

4. Large number of buyers and sellers exist in the market and there is tough competition.

Question 3. Describe the four major sectors in an economy according to the macroeconomics point of view.

Answer According to the macroeconomics an economy in classified into the following four sectors

1. **Household Sector** This sector engaged in the consumption of goods and services. Household spend their income on payment for goods and services purchased, payment of tax to government.

2. **Production Sector** This sector engaged in the production of goods and services. This sector makes payments for factor services to households, taxes to the government, imports of the materials.

3. **Government Sector** This sector engaged in such activities which are related to taxation and subsidies.

4. **Rest of the World Sector** This sector engaged in imports and exports. It makes payments for import of goods and services, for factor services to the household.

Question 4. Describe the Great Depression of 1929.

Answer The Great Depression was an immense tragedy in 1929. There was a severe economic crisis took place in the United States the day when the stock market crashed. Masses of people tried to sell their stock but nobody was ready to purchase.

It effected the other countries also. The main cause behind it was the fall of aggregate demand due to under consumption and over investment. The demand for goods in the economy was so low that the production was lowered and leading to unemployment. In USA the rate of unemployment increased from 3% to 25%.

2

National Income Accounting

Points to Remember

1. **Final Goods** These are those goods which have crossed the boundary line of production and are ready for use by their final users.

   Final goods are often classified as
   (i) Final consumer goods
   (ii) Final producer goods

2. **Intermediate Goods** These are those goods which have yet not crossed the boundary line of production.

   Example Shirts purchased by firm x from firm y for resale are intermediate goods.

3. **Consumption Goods** These are those goods which are directly used for the satisfaction of human wants. These are not used in the production of other goods.

   Example Ice cream and milk used by the households. Consumption goods are classified into four categories.
   (i) Durable Consumer Goods: TV, radio, car etc.
   (ii) Semi-Durable Consumer Goods: Clothes, furnitures etc.
   (iii) Non-Durable Consumer Goods: Bread.
   (iv) Services: Doctor, lawyer etc.

4. **Capital Goods** These are those goods which are used in the process of production for several years and which are of high value.

   Example Plant and machinery

5. **Investment** Investment is a process of capital formation, or a process of increase in the stock of capital.

   Investment has two components

   (i) Fixed investment　　　　　(ii) Inventory investment

6. **Gross Investment** Expenditure on the purchase of fixed assets during the accounting year.
   + Expenditure on the inventory stock during the accounting year.

7. **Net Investment** Gross investment – Depreciation (Consumption of fixed capital)

8. **Stock** A stock is a quantity of any economic variable which is measured at a particular point of time. *e.g.,* 100 crores population of India in 2001.

9. **Flow** A flow is a quantity of any economic variable which is measured during a period of time. *e.g.,* Monthly wages of a worker.

10. **Depreciation** Depreciation refers to loss of value of fixed assets in use on account of

    (i) Normal wear tear

    (ii) Normal rate of accidental changes

    (iii) Expected or foreseen obsolesencene

    Annual amount of depreciation

    $$= \frac{\text{Original value of the machine}}{\text{Number of years of the life of the machine}}$$

11. **Circular Flow of Income** It refers to the unending flow of the activities of production, income generation and expenditure involving different sectors of the economy.

    There are three phases of circular flow

    (i) Production　　　(ii) Income generation　　　(iii) Expenditure

12. **Money Flow** It refers to the flow of money across different sectors of the economy.

13. **Real Flow** It refers to the flow of goods and services across different sectors of the economy.

14. **Condition for Equilibrium in Four Sector Economy**

    $$C + S + T = C + I + G + (X - M)$$

    Here, C = Consumption; S = Saving

    I = Investment; T = Tax revenue; G = Government expenditure

    X = Exports; M = Import; $(X - M)$ = Net Exports

15. **Injection** It refers to the additions to the circular flow injections causes expension of the circular flow.

    Example   Government expenditure, export and investment.

16. **Leakages**   It refers to the withdrawl's from the circular flow leakages cause contraction of the circular flow.

17. **Normal Residents of a Country**   These are the people who
    (i) normally reside in the country concerned and
    (ii) whose centre of economic interest lies in the country concerned.

18. **Domestic Territory of a Country**   It refers to that area of economic activity which generates domestic income.

19. **Factor Incomes**   These are the income received by the owners of factors of production for rendering their factor services to the producer.

20. **Transfer Payment**   These are all those unilateral payments corresponding to which there is no value-addition in the economy.

    Example   Gifts, donations etc.

21. **Methods of Measurement of National Income**
    (i)   Product or Value Added Method
    (ii) Income Method
    (iii) Expenditure Method

22. **Value Added**   Value of output – Intermediate consumption
    (i) Value of output = sales + change in stock
    (ii) Change in stock = closing stock – opening stock

23. **Planned Change in Inventories**   It means that the actual change in inventories is just equal to what was planned.

24. **Unplanned Change in Inventories**   Unexpected rise in inventories during a year is termed as unplanned change in inventories.

25. **Components of Domestic Factor Income**
    (i) **Compensation to Employees**   It includes following components-wages and salaries in cash, compensation in kind, employer's contributions to social security scheme.
    (ii) **Operating Surplus**   It has two main components
        (a) Income from property
        (b) Income from entrepreneurship
    (iii) Mixed income of the self employed

26. **Final Expenditure**   The main components of final expenditure are
    (i) Private final consumption expenditure

    (ii) Gross domestic capital formation

    (iii) Government final consumption expenditure

    (iv) Net export (X-M)

27. **National Income**   It is sum total of factor incomes accruing to the normal residents of a country.

28. **Domestic Income**   It is the sum total of factor income generated with in the domestic territory of the country no matter it is the income accruing to residents or non-residents of the country.

29. **National Income at Current Price**   It is the money value of all final goods and services measured at current prices.

30. **GDP**   It is the sum total of

    (i) Compensation of employees

    (ii) Operating surplus

    (iii) Mixed income

    (iv) Consumption of fixed capital with in the domestic territory of the country during the period of one year.

31. **NNP at Market Price**   It refers to the market value of final goods and services produced during the year inclusive of net factor income from abroad but exclusive of depreciation.

32. **NNP at Factor Cost**   It is the sum total of factor incomes earned by normal residents of a country during the period of one year.

33. **Private Income**   It is the total income from all sources that accrues to the private sector during the period of one year.

34. **Personal Income**   It is the income actually received by the individuals and households from all sources in the form of current transfer payment and factor incomes.

35. **Personal Disposable Income**   It is the personal income remaining with individuals after deduction of all taxes levied against their income and their property as well as payment miscellaneous fees and fines.

36. **National Disposable Income**   It is the income from all sources available to residents of a country for consumption expenditure or for saving during a year.

37. **Nominal GDP**   It refers to GDP at current price.

38. **Real GDP**   It refers to GDP at constant price.

39. **GNP Deflator**   The GNP deflator measures the average level of the prices of all goods and services that make-up GNP. GNP deflator is measured as the ratio of nominal GNP to real GNP.

40. **Consumer Price Index** (CPI)   This is the index of prices of a given basket   of commodities which are bought by the representative consumer. CPI is generally expressed in percentage terms.

41. **Externalities**   It refers to the benefits a firm or an individual causes to another for which they are not paid.

QR Code Questions

Question 1. Fill in the correct options from the following

Income per person, compares the income level of different countries, the increase of wealthy class per capita above the majority population

(i) PCI .....

(ii) Purchasing Power Parity.......

(iii) If the Income Distribution is Skewed ....

Answer

(i) Income per person

(ii) Compares the Income level of different countries

(iii) The increase of Wealthy class per capita above the majority population

Question 2. Per Capita Income is .... of the country.

(a) disposable income   (b) average income
(c) real income   (d) private income

Answer   (b) Average income

Question 3. Narrow money includes

(a) $M_1 + M_2$ (b) $M_1 + M_3$
(c) $M_2 + M_3$ (d) M_4

Answer   (a) $M_1 + M_2$

This concept is explained in Chapter-3 (Part-B) of NCERT Book.

Question 4. In circular flow of income, export is considered as......

(a) spending   (b) injection
(c) income   (d) leakages

Answer   (b) injection

Question 5. .... is the leakage from the circular flow of income.

    (a) Saving   (b) Government Spending

    (c) Export   (d) Investment

Answer (a) Saving

Question 6. Financial help to a patient is ....

    (a) net factor income   (b) net factor income from abroad

    (c) transfer payments   (d) factor income

Answer (c) Transfer payments

Question 7. National income is also called ....

    (a) NNP at MP   (b) NDP at FC   (c) NDP at MP   (d) NNP at FC

Answer (d) NNP at FC

Question 8. Which sector has the maximum share in the National Income of India?

    (a) Tertiary sector   (b) Secondary sector

    (c) Primary sector

Answer (a) Tertiary sector

Question 9.

Black money implies ......

    (a) income on which payment of tax is usually evaded

    (b) counterfeit currency

    (c) money earned through underhand deals

    (d) All of the above

Answer (a) income on which payment of tax is usually evaded

     This concept is explained in Chapter-3 (Part-B) of NCERT Book.

Question 10.

What is the rank of India in International Corruption Perception Index 2017?

    (a) 80   (b) 82   (c) 79   (d) 81

Answer (c) 79

Exercises

Question 1. What are the four factors of production and what are the remunerations to each of these called?

Answer The four factors of productions are

1. **Land** It is a free gift of nature and it is called as natural, original or primary factor of production.
2. **Labour** It is a person engaged in some physical work it is the human factor of production.
3. **Capital** It means wealth, money or income which is invested in business it helps in the production function.
4. **Entrepreneur** It is the work of an entrepreneur to bring the required factors together and work harmoniously.

The remuneration to them are as follows

1. **Land** Rent is a reward for the use of land.
2. **Labour** Wages are the reward for a labour.
3. **Capital** Interest is the reward for capital.
4. **Entrepreneur** Profit is the reward for an entrepreneur.

Question 2. Why should the aggregate final expenditure of an economy be equal to the aggregate factor payments? Explain.

Answer In a simplified economy, income is either spent on the purchase of final goods and services or saved. Expenditure of income on the final goods either causes final consumption expenditure or investment expenditure.

To the extent income is saved, final goods remain unsold. But it treated as inventory investment. So it is said that aggregate final expenditure of an economy is equal to aggregate factor payments. *i.e.,* $Y = C + S$

Question 3. Distinguish between stock and flow. Between net investment and capital which is a stock and which is a flow? Compare net investment and capital with flow of water into a tank.

Answer Difference between Stock and Flow

S.No.	Stock	Flow
1.	Stock refers to that variable, which is measured at a particular point of time.	Flow refers to that variable which is measured over a period of time.
2.	It does not have a time dimension.	It has a time dimension.
3.	It is a static concept.	It is a dynamic concept.
4.	Examples-1-Stock of goods in the godown, National Wealth, National Capital, Money supply etc.	Examples-National Income, Expenditure, Number of births during a particular year etc.

Difference between Net Investment and Capital

S.No.	Net Investment	Capital
1.	Net investment is a gross investment minus depreciation of the fixed assets, net investment causes net addition to the stock of capital.	Capital is the income which is used in the process of productions like plant and machinery.
2.	Net investment is a flow variable	Capital is a stock variable.

Flow of water in a tank is a flow concept because it is measured in per unit of time period. Whereas, stock of water in a tank is stock because it is measured at a point of time. Capital is like a stock of water in the tank at a point of time.

Question 4. What is the difference between planned and unplanned inventory accumulation? Write down the relation between change in inventories and value added of a firm.

Answer In case of an expected fall in sales, the firm will have unsold stock of goods which had not anticipated. Hence, there will be planned accumulation of inventories, whereas in case of an unexpected fall in sales, the firm have unsold goods which it had not anticipated. Hence, there will be unplanned accumulation of inventories.

Relation between Change in Inventories and Value Added Change in inventories of a firm during a year = value added + intermediate goods used by the firm – sale of the firm during a year and value added in net contribution made by a firm in the process of production. It is value added = value of production – value of intermediate goods used.

Question 5. Write down the three identities of calculating the GDP of a country by the three methods. Also briefly explain why each of these should give us the same value of GDP.

Answer Three identities of calculating GDP are as follows

I. **Product Method or Value Added Method** It is that method which measures national income in terms of value addition by each producing enterprise in the economy. It is calculated as
Gross Value Added in the primary sector at Market Price + Gross Value Added in the secondary sector at Market Price + Gross Value Added in the tertiary sector at Market Price $= GDP_{MP}$

$$GDP_{MP} - \text{Depreciation} = \text{Net Domestic Product at Market Price}$$

$$NDP_{MP} - \text{Net Indirect Tax} = \text{Net Domestic Product at Factor Cost}$$

$$NDP_{FC} + NFIA = \text{National Income}$$

II. **Income Method** Under this method national income is measured in terms of factor payments to the owners of factors of production. It is calculated as

Compensation of Employees + Operating Surplus + Mixed Income of the self employed = Net Domestic Income
Net Domestic Income + NFIA = National Income

III. **Expenditure Method** Under this method national income is measured in terms of expenditure on the purchase of final goods and services produced in the economy. it is calculated as

Private Final Consumption Expenditure + Government Final Consumption Expenditure + Gross Domestic Fixed Capital Formation + Change in Stock + Net Exports $= GDP_{MP}$

$$GDP_{MP} - \text{Depreciation} = \text{Net Domestic Product}_{MP}$$

$$NDP_{MP} - \text{Net Indirect Tax} = NDP_{FC}$$

$$NDP_{FC} + NFIA = \text{National Income}$$

Question 6. Define budget deficit and trade deficit. The excess of private investment over saving of a country in a particular year was ₹ 2,000 crores. The amount of budget deficit was $(-)$ ₹ 1,500 crores. What was the volume of trade deficit of that country?

Answer **Budget Deficit** Budget deficit refers to the situation when amount of the governments expenditure exceeds the tax revenue earned by government.

Trade Deficit Trade deficit is the excess of import expenditure over the export revenue earned by the economy.

$$\text{Trade Deficit} = M - X \quad \text{or} \quad (I - S) + (G - T)$$

M (Outflow from the country) *I* (Investment) × (Inflow into the country) *S* (Saving) *G – T* (Budget Deficit).
It is given

$$I - S = 2{,}000 \text{ crores}$$
$$G - T = (-)\,1{,}500 \text{ crores}$$
$$\text{Trade Deficit} = 2{,}000 + (-1{,}500) = ₹\,500 \text{ crores}$$

Question 7. Suppose the GDP at market price of a country in a particular year ₹ 1,100 crores. Net Factor Income from Abroad was ₹ 100 crores. The value of Indirect taxes–Subsidies was ₹ 150 crores and National Income was ₹ 850 crores. Calculate the aggregate value of depreciation.

Answer

$$\text{Given- } GDP_{MP} = 1{,}100 \text{ crores}, \ NFIA = 100 \text{ crores}$$
$$NIT = 150 \text{ crores}, \ NNP_{FC} = ₹\,850 \text{ crores}$$
$$\therefore \quad GDP_{FC} = GDP_{MP} - NIT = 1{,}100 - 150 = ₹\,950 \text{ crores}$$
$$GNP_{FC} = GDP_{FC} + NFIA = 950 + 100 = ₹\,1{,}050 \text{ crores}$$
$$GNP_{FC} = NNP_{FC} + \text{Depreciation}$$
$$1{,}050 = 850 + \text{Depreciation}$$
$$\text{Depreciation} = 1{,}050 - 850 = ₹\,200 \text{ crores}$$

Question 8. Net National Product at Factor Cost of a particular country in a year is ₹ 1,900 crores. There are no interest payments made by the households to the firms/government or by the firms/government to the households. The personal disposable income of the households is ₹ 1,200 crores. The personal income taxes paid by them is ₹ 600 crores and the value of retained earnings of the firms and government is valued at ₹ 200 crores. What is the value of transfer payments made by the government and firms to the households?

Answer Given, Personal Disposable Income (PDI) = ₹ 1,200 crores

$$\text{Personal Taxes (Direct tax)} = 600 \text{ crores}$$
$$\text{Personal Income} = PDI + \text{Direct taxes}$$
$$= 1{,}200 + 600 = ₹\,1{,}800 \text{ crores}$$
$$\text{Private Income} = \text{Personal income} + \text{Retained saving}$$
$$= 1{,}800 + 200 = ₹\,2{,}000 \text{ crores}$$
$$\therefore \quad NNP_{FC} = \text{Private income} - \text{Transfer payments}$$
$$1{,}900 = 2{,}000 - TP$$
$$TP = ₹\,100 \text{ crores}$$
$$\text{Value of Transfer Payment} = ₹\,100 \text{ crores}$$

Question 9. From the following data, calculate Personal Income and Personal Disposable Income.

		₹ (Crore)
(a)	Net Domestic Product at Factor Cost	8,000
(b)	Net Factor Income from Abroad	200
(c)	Undisbursed Profit	1,000
(d)	Corporate Tax	500
(e)	Interest Received by Households	1,500
(f)	Interest Paid by Households	1,200
(g)	Transfer Income	300
(h)	Personal Tax	500

Answer

$$\text{Private Income} = \text{Net Domestic Product} + \text{NFIA}$$
$$+ \text{Transfer payment} + \text{Interest received}$$
$$= 8,000 + 200 + 300 + 1,500 = ₹\ 10,000 \text{ crores}$$
$$\text{Personal Income} = \text{Private income} - \text{Undistributed Profit}$$
$$- \text{Corporate Tax}$$
$$= 10,000 - 500 - 1,000 = ₹\ 8,500 \text{ crores}$$
$$\text{Personal Disposal Income} = \text{Personal income} - \text{Direct tax} - \text{Interest paid}$$
$$= 8,500 - 500 - 1,200 = ₹\ 6,800 \text{ crores}$$

Question 10. In a single day Raju, the barber, collects ₹ 500 from haircuts; over this day, his equipment depreciates in value by ₹ 50. Of the remaining ₹ 450, Raju pays sales tax worth ₹ 30, takes home ₹ 200 and retains ₹ 220 for improvement and buying of new equipment. He further pays ₹ 20 as income tax from his income. Based on this information, complete Raju's contribution to the following measures of income (a) Gross Domestic Product (b) NNP at Market Price (c) NNP at Factor Cost (d) Personal Income (e) Personal Disposable Income.

Answer   Given Indirect taxes = ₹ 30, Personal tax = ₹ 20

Depreciation ₹ 50, Retained earnings = ₹ 220

$$\therefore \quad GDP_{MP} = ₹\ 500$$
$$NNP_{MP} = GDP_{MP} - \text{Depreciation}$$
$$= 500 - 50 = ₹\ 450$$
$$NNP_{FC} = NNP_{MP} - NIT$$
$$= 450 - 30 = ₹\ 420$$

$$\text{Personal Income} = NNP_{FC} - \text{Retained earning}$$
$$= 420 - 220 = ₹\ 200$$
$$\text{Personal Disposable Income} = \text{Personal Income} - \text{Direct tax}$$
$$= 200 - 20 = ₹\ 180$$

Question 11. The value of the nominal GNP of an economy was ₹ 2,500 crores in a particular year. The value of GNP of that country during the same year, evaluated at the prices of same base year, was ₹ 3,000 crores. Calculate the value of the GNP deflator of the year in percentage terms. Has the price level risen between the base year and the year under consideration?

Answer $\text{GNP Deflator} = \dfrac{\text{Nominal GNP}}{\text{Real GNP}} \times 100 = \dfrac{2,500}{3,000} \times 100 = 83.33\%$

No, the price level has fallen down by 16.67%.

Question 12. Write down some of the limitations of using GDP as an index of welfare of a country.

Answer   Followings are the limitations of using GDP as an index of welfare of a country.

(i) With every increase in the level of GDP, distribution of GDP is getting more unequal, welfare level of the society may not rise.

(ii) Composition of GDP may not be welfare oriented even when the level of GDP tends to rise.

(iii) Because of non-monetary transactions GDP remains under estimated, and is therefore not a proper index of welfare.

(iv) Impact of externalities (positive or negative impact of an activity) is not accounted in the index of social welfare in terms of GDP.

3

Money and Banking

Points to Remember

1. **Barter System**   Barter system means the direct exchange of one commodity to another.

2. **Barter Economy** can be termed as C-C economy *i.e.,* Commodity for Commodity economy.

3. **Difficulties of Barter System**
   (i) Lack of double coincidence
   (ii) Lack of divisibility
   (iii) Lack of common measure
   (iv) Difficulty of storage and transfer of wealth
   (v) Difficulty in deferred payment
   (vi) Difficulty in the exchange of services

4. **Money**   Money is anything that is generally acceptable as a means of exchange and at the same time, act as a measure and as a store of value.

   According to **Walker**, "Money is what money does".

5. **Functions of Money**
   (i) **Primary Function**

      (a) Medium of exchange   (b) Measure of value
   (ii) **Secondary Function of Money**

      (a) Standard of deferred payments
      (b) Store of value
      (c) Transfer of value

(iii) **Contingent Functions**

    (a) Distribution of national income

    (b) Maximum satisfaction to the consumers

    (c) Maximum profit to the producers

    (d) Basis of credit

    (e) Liquidity

6. **Fiat Money** It refers to money by order/authority of the government. It includes notes and coins.

7. **Fiduciary Money** It refers to money backed up by trust between the payer and the payee.

8. **Money Supplier** In the modern times, the sources of supply of money are government, central bank of the country and commercial banks.

9. **High Powered Money** It includes currency (R) with the public and cash (c) reserves with banks.

High powerd money $= R + c$

10. **Banking** Banking implies accepting deposits of money from the public for the purpose of lending or investment which is repayable on demand and can be withdrawn by means of cheques, draft order etc.

11. **Commercial Bank** A commercial bank is a financial institution engaged in the business of accepting deposits and making loans to the people.

12. **Central Bank** A central bank is an apex institution of a country that controls and regulates the monetary and financial system of the country.

13. **Functions of Commercial Banks**

    (i) Acceptance of deposits from the public

    (ii) Advancing of loans

    (iii) Investment of funds

    (iv) Agency functions

        (a) Remittance of funds

        (b) Collection and payment of fund

        (c) Sale and purchase of security

        (d) Representation and correspondence

        (e) Trusteeship

    (v) General utility functions

    (vi) Credit creation

14. **Factors Affecting Credit Creation**
    (i) Primary cash deposits
    (ii) Cash reserve ratio
    (iii) Banking habits of the people
    (iv) Policy of the central

15. **Functions of Central Banks** (RBI)
    (i) Bank of issue
    (ii) Banker, agent and advisor to the government
    (iii) Custodian of the cash reserves of commercial banks
    (iv) Custodian of nation's reserves of international currency
    (v) Lender of the last resort
    (vi) Bank of central clearance
    (vii) Controller of money supply and credit

16. **Instruments of Monetary Policy or Credit Control Measures**
    (i) **Quantitative Instruments**
        (a) Bank rate
        (b) Open market operation
        (c) Cash Reserve Ratio (CRR)
        (d) Statutory Liquidity Ratio (SLR)
    (ii) **Qualitative Instruments**
        (a) Margin requirement
        (b) Rationing of credit
        (c) Direct action
        (d) Moral suasion

17. **Cash Reserve Ratio** (CRR) It refers to the minimum percentage of a bank's total deposits required to be kept with the central bank.

18. **Statutory Liquidity Ratio** (SLR) Every bank is required to maintain a fixed percentage of its assets in the form of cash or other liquid assets.

QR Code Questions

Question 1. If the RBI increases the CRR, banks will have....... (more / less) money to lend.

Answer less

Question 2. Find the components of a Cheque.

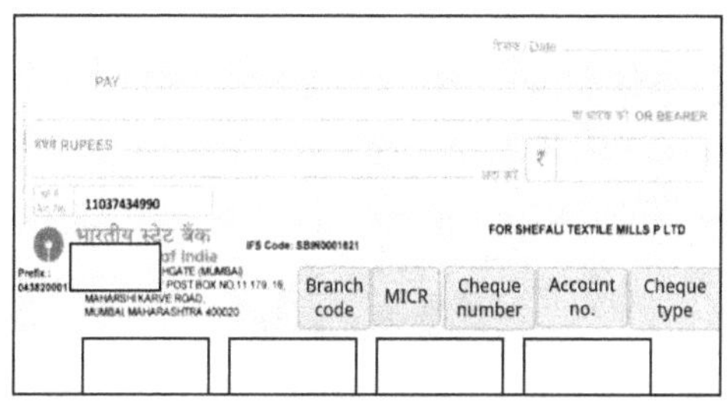

Answer Branch code, Cheque number, MICR, Account no., Cheque type

Question 3. Mention the correct year of each from the following 1964, 1935, 1950, 1982

(i) RBI ......

(ii) NABARD.......

(iii) Planning Commission......

(iv) FCI ....

Answer (i) 1935   (ii) 1982   (iii) 1950   (iv) 1964

Question 4. Identify the logo

(a) ICICI bank   (b) Dena Bank
(c) HDFC bank   (d) State Bank of India

Answer (a) ICICI bank

Question 5. Identify the logo

(a) Indian overseas bank
(b) HDFC bank
(c) Dena Bank
(d) Punjab National Bank

Answer   (a) Indian overseas bank

Question 6. Identify the logo

(a) Union Bank of India
(b) State Bank of India
(c) HDFC Bank
(d) Dena Bank

Answer   (b) State Bank of India

Question 7. Identify the logo

(a) Oriental Bank of commerce
(b) Union Bank of India
(c) State Bank of India
(d) Dena Bank

Answer   (b) Union Bank of India

Question 8. Fill in the correct full forms of the Organisations

(i) RBI   (ii) SBI   (iii) NABARD   (iv) LIC

Answer
(i) Reserve Bank of India
(ii) State Bank of India
(iii) National Bank for Agriculture and Rural Development
(iv) Life Insurance Corporation of India

Question 9.

The delivery of financial services to the weaker sections and low-income groups at an affordable cost is called financial exclusion.

    (a) True   (b) False

Answer (b) False. The delivery of financial services to the weaker sections and low-income groups at an affordable cost is called financial inclusion.

Question 10. Which bank opened customer service points to extend financial inclusion, targeting the urban poor?

    (a) SBI   (b) PNB

    (c) IDBI   (d) HDFC

Answer (a) SBI

Question 11. Fill in the missing word.

As per CRISIL index on financial inclusion....... part of India is at the top in financial inclusion.

Answer central

Exercises

Question 1. What is a barter system? What are its drawbacks?

Answer **Barter System** Barter system refers to the exchange of goods for goods.

e.g., If a person exchange wheat with rice. It is a barter system.

Drawbacks of Barter system are as follows

1. **Difficulty of Double Coincidence of Wants** It is not necessary that goods in possession of two different individuals are needed by each other.

2. **Lack of a Common Unit of Value** It implies that the goods which are exchanged not measured in a common unit.

3. **Lack of a System for Future Payments** Evolution is difficult thus future payments would not be possible.

Question 2. What are the main functions of money? How does money overcome the shortcomings of a barter system?

Answer The functions of money can be divided in two categories–
1. Primary or (Main functions)
2. Secondary functions

I. The primary functions are of two types

   1. **Medium of Exchange** It can be used to make payment for all transactions of goods and services.

   2. **Measure of Value** It means that the value of each goods and services are measured in the monetary unit.

II. Secondary functions are of three types

   1. **Deferred Payments** Money is used to make the future payments.

   2. **Store of Value** It implies store of wealth.

   3. **Transfer of Value** Money is used as a convenient mode of transfer of value.

The money over comes from the short comings of the barter system in a following manner

   (a) Use of money removed the difficulty of double coincidence of wants in the barter system.

   (b) Money facilitates storage of value.

   (c) Use of money removed the difficulty of division of commodity.

   (d) It removed the difficulty of medium of exchange.

   (e) Use of money removed the difficulty of deferred payments.

Question 3. What is transaction demand for money? How is it related to the value of transactions over a specified period of time?

Answer The transaction motive relates to the demand for money to meet day-to-day transactions.

According to **Keynes**, "Transaction demand for money is positively associated with the level of income, as higher the level of income, larger would be the size of money holdings for transactions. The relationship between the value of transactions and transaction demand is

$$M_T^d = KT \quad \text{or} \quad \frac{1}{K} M_T^d = T \quad \text{or} \quad VM_T^d = T$$

$$V = \frac{1}{K} \text{, represents velocity of circulation of money.}$$

Here, T = Total value of transactions of money; K = Positive fractions

   M_T^d = Stock of money hold by people

Question 4. What are the alternative definitions of money supply in India?

Answer There are four alternative measures of money supply in India. These are known as

M_1, M_2, M_3 and M_4 define as

$M_1 \Rightarrow$ Currency with public + Demand deposits + Other deposits with RBI

$M_2 \Rightarrow M_1 +$ Saving with post office saving account

$M_3 \Rightarrow M_1 +$ Net time deposits with banks

$M_4 \Rightarrow M_3 +$ Total deposits with post office (except NSC)

Question 5. What is a 'legal tender'? What is 'fiat money'?

Answer Legal Tender Legal tender refers to the money which can be legally used to make payment of debts or other obligations.

Fiat Money Fiat money refers to the money which is backed with order of the government under law. It must be accepted for all debts.

Question 6. What is high powered money?

Answer High Power Money It means currency (coins and notes) held by the public and cash reserves with the commercial banks.

Question 7. Explain the functions of a commercial bank.

Answer Function of Commercial Bank

The function of commercial bank divided into three categories

(i) **Primary Functions** A commercial bank performs two primary functions

    (a) **Accepting Deposits** Commercial bank accepts deposits from public by several kinds of account like

        (a) Current account   (b) Fixed deposit account

        (c) Saving account   (d) Reccuring deposit account

    (b) **Providing Loans and Advances** A commercial bank provides loans and advances both for productive purpose as well as consumption (household) purpose. The commercial bank provides–cash credit, demand loans and short term loans.

(ii) **Secondary Functions** In addition to the primary functions, banks also perform the following secondary functions

    (a) **Overdraft Facility** It refers to a facility in which a account holder is allowed to overdraw amount upto limit from his current account.

    (b) **Discounting Bills of Exchange** The commercial bank provides the facility of discounting bill before the date of maturity.

(iii) **Agency Functions** A commercial bank acts as an agent of his customer. Some of the agency functions are

(a) Transfer of funds.

(b) Collection and payment of various items.

(c) Purchase and sale of foreign exchange.

(d) Purchase and sale of securities

(e) Act as consultant.

(f) Provide locker facility.

(g) Provide information and statistics data to the customers.

Question 8. What is money multiplier? What determines the value of this multiplier?

Answer Money multiplier measures the amount of money that the banks are able to create in the form of deposits with each unit of money it keeps as reserves. Its value is determined in ratio of total money supply to the stock of the high powered money in an economy, as

$$\text{Money multiplier} = \frac{M}{H} = \frac{1 + cdr}{cdr + rdr} > 1$$

$$rdr < 1$$

The currency deposit ratio (cdr) and reserve deposit ratio (rdr) plays an important role in determining money multiplier.

cdr is the ratio of money held by the public.

$$cdr = \frac{C}{DD} \quad \text{ratio of the total deposit kept by commercial banks.}$$

rdr is the proportion of the total deposit kept by commercial banks.

Question 9. What are the instruments of monetary policy of RBI?

Answer Following are the instruments of monetary policy of RBI

(i) **Quantitative Instrument** It affects the overall supply of money and credit in the economy. These instruments are

(a) **Bank Rate** The rate at which RBI gives credit to the commercial banks. A low or high banks rate encourages banks to keep small proportion of their deposits as reserve which in result either reduce the flow of credit or increase the flow of credit.

(b) **Open Market Operations** It refers to the sale or purchase of securities by RBI in the open market.

(c) **Reserve Ratios** Ratios like CRR (Credit Reserve Ratio) (Statutory Liquid Ratio) SLR are playing an important role as the quantitative instrument.

(ii) **Qualitative Instrument** These instruments direct or restrict the flow of credit to the specified areas of economic activity. These instruments are

(a) **Margin Requirements** It refers to the difference between the current value of the security offered for loans and value of loans granted.

(b) **Rationing of Credit** It refers to the fixation of quotas for different business activities.

(c) **Moral Suasion** It implies informal suggestion by the RBI to commercial banks to co-operate with the general monetary policy.

Question 10. Do you consider a commercial bank 'creator of money' in the economy?

Answer Yes, commercial bank acts as a creator of money in the economy. They create credit in the form of demand deposit related to the loans offered by them. Thus, banks create credit by advancing loans.

Question 11. What role of RBI is known as lender of last resort?

Answer When commercial bank fails to get their financial requirements from other sources in the market, then they approach the RBI (central bank). The central bank gives loan to commercial banks . This situation termed as a lender of the last resort. The central bank ensures that the banking system does not suffer any set-back and money market remains stable.

4

Determination of Income and Employment

Points to Remember

1. **Aggregate Demand** (AD) It refers to the total demand for final goods and services in an economy during a year.

    (i) Components of Aggregate Demand

      (a) Private consumption demand (C)

      (b) Private investment demand (I)

      (c) Demand for goods and services by the government or government purchases (G)

      (d) Demand for net exports (X-M)

    Thus, $AD = C + I + G + NE$

2. **Aggregate Supply** (AS) It refers to the total quantity of goods and services produced by all the producers in an economy during a year.

    (i) Components of Aggregate Supply

      (a) Consumption (C)   (b) Saving (S)

    Thus, $AS = C + S$

3. **Consumption Function** It means a functional relationship between total consumption and total disposable income.

    Thus, $C = f(y)$

      C = Consumption; Y = Income

4. **Average Propensity to Consume** $\text{APC} = \dfrac{C}{Y}$

   C = Total consumption; Y = Total income

5. Marginal Propensity to Consume (MPC)

$$\text{MPC} = \dfrac{\Delta c}{\Delta y}$$

   Here, Δc = Change in consumption; Δy = Change in income

6. **Linear Consumption Function** If the consumption function is given on the assumption of constant marginal propensity to consume. It is called linear consumption function.

   $c = \bar{c} + BY; \qquad \bar{c} > 0, 0 < b < 1$

   Here, c = Consumption

   $\bar{c}$ = Autonomous consumption

   B = Marginal propensity to consume

   Y = Level of income

7. **Saving Function** Saving function is a schedule showing a functional relationship between total saving and total income.

   Thus, $S = F(Y)$

   Here, S = Total saving; Y = Total income

8. **Average Propensity to Save**

   $\text{APS} = \dfrac{S}{Y}$

   Here, S = Total saving; Y = Total income

9. **Marginal Propensity to Save**

   $\text{MPS} = \dfrac{\Delta S}{\Delta Y}$

   Here, ΔS = Change in saving; Δy = Change in income

10. **Equilibrium Level of Output** Equilibrium level of output in an economy is determined at a point where planned spending (C+I) equals the planned output or where C+I curve intersects the 45° line.

11. **Effective Demand** It is that level of aggregate demand which becomes effective in determining equilibrium level of income because it is equal to aggregate supply.

12. **Autonomous Consumption** It refers to minimum level of consumption even when income is zero, it is indicated by 'A' in the consumption function

$$C = A + B$$

13. **Ex-ante Saving** It is what the savers plan to save at different levels of income in the economy.

14. **Ex-ante Investment** Is what the investors plan or intend to invest at different levels of income in the economy.

15. **Ex-post Saving and Investment** They refer to realised saving and investment in the economy. Ex-post saving is always equal to ex-post investment.

16. **Multiplier** Additional investment (ΔI), generates additional income (ΔY), but income generated is many times more than the investment. Multiplier is the ratio between increase in income (ΔY) and increase in investment (ΔI)

$$\text{Multiplier } (K) = \frac{\Delta Y}{\Delta I}$$

17. **Full Employment Equilibrium** It refers to that situation in the economy when $AD = AS$ along with fuller utilisation of labour force.

18. **Under Employment Equilibrium** It refers to that situation in the economy when $AS = AD$ but without the fuller utilisation of labour force.

19. **Parodox of Thrift** Which states that as people become more thrift they end up saving less or same as before.

QR Code Questions

Question 1. An increase in the MPC will

    (a) shift the consumption function downwards.
    (b) shift the consumption function upwards.
    (c) shift the saving function upwards.
    (d) lead to a steeper slope of consumption function.

Answer   (b) shift the consumption function upwards.

Question 2. Which of the following is the cause of Inflation?

    (a) An increase in CRR
    (b) Deficit Financing
    (c) Rise in Loans
    (d) Unfavourable BOP

Answer   (b) Deficit Financing

Question 3. If GDP is falling and unemployment rate is rising, which of the following fiscal policy measures should government take?
    (a) To decrease spending
    (b) To decrease taxes
    (c) To increase money supply
    (d) To decrease reserve requirement

Answer (b) To decrease taxes

Question 4. If the net exports are positive, the aggregate demand curve will
    (a) Shift to right   (b) No effect
    (c) Shift to left   (d) Shift downward

Answer (a) Shift to right

Question 5.

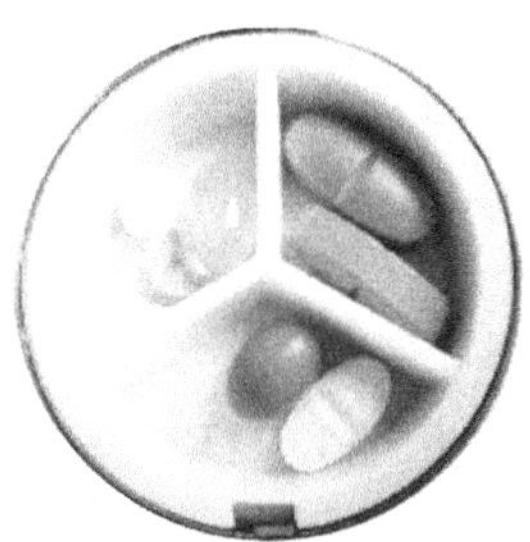

What is the current FDI (Foreign Direct Investment) percentage limit in the Pharmaceutical industry in India?
    (a) 74   (b) 39
    (c) 50   (d) 49

Answer (a) 74

Question 6. What is the current FDI percentage limit in Tourism?
    (a) 50   (b) 23
    (c) 100   (d) 26

Answer (c) 100

Question 7. FDI is not allowed in which among the following sectors in India?
    (a) Pharmacy   (b) Railway
    (c) Defence   (d) Atomic Energy

Answer (d) Atomic Energy

Question 8. What is the full form of FDI?
- (a) Free Direct Investment
- (b) Foreign Distance Investment
- (c) Full Direct Investment
- (d) Foreign Direct Investment

Answer (d) Foreign Direct Investment

Question 9. What is the full form of CRR?
- (a) Cash Reserve Ratio
- (b) Credit Reserve Ratio
- (c) Credit Retrogate Ratio
- (d) Central Reserve Ratio

Answer (a) Cash Reserve Ratio

Question 10. What is full form of SEZ?
- (a) Social Economy Zone
- (b) Special Economic Zone
- (c) Special Economy Zone
- (d) Social Engineering Zone

Answer (b) Special Economic Zone

Question 11. What is full form of SLR?
- (a) Statutory Liquidity Ratio
- (b) Sum Liquidity Ratio
- (c) Sum Liquid Ratio
- (d) Social Liquidity Ratio

Answer (a) Statutory Liquidity Ratio

Exercises

Question 1. What is marginal propensity to consume? How is it related to marginal propensity to save?

Answer Marginal propensity to consume is the ratio of change in consumption expenditure to change in total income.

$$MPC = \frac{\Delta C}{\Delta Y}$$

Marginal propensity to save refers to the ratio of change in saving to change in income

$$MPS = \frac{\Delta S}{\Delta Y}$$

Marginal propensity to consume and marginal propensity to save is equal to one or MPC = 1 – MPS, MPS = 1 – MPC

$$MPC + MPS = 1$$

Here MPS = Marginal Propensity to Save

MPC = Marginal Propensity to Consume

ΔC = Change in consumption expenditure

ΔY = Change in total income; ΔS = Change in saving

Question 2.   What is difference between ex-ante investment and ex-post investment?

Answer   Ex-ante investment is the amount of investment which firms plan to invest at different level of income in the economy, whereas ex-post investment is the amount realised or actual investment in an economy during a year.

Question 3. What do you understand by parametric shift of a line? How does a line shift when its

(i) slope decreases   (ii) its intercept increases?

Answer   Parametric shift is a graph due to change in the value of a parameter.

(i) A positively sloping straight line swings upwards at its slope is decreases.

(ii) A positively sloping straight line shifts upwards in parallel as its intercept is increased.

Question 4. What is effective demand? How will you derive the autonomous expenditure multiplier when price of final goods and the rate of interest are given?

Answer   It in an economy as people become more thrifty they end up saving less or same as before in aggregate. This theory produced by Keynes "When people start saving money instead of spending it, in response to growing concerns about a recession, they actually make the recession worse."

Rise in MPS means a fall in MPC. When MPC falls, aggregate consumption expenditure in the economy falls. It leads to rise in inventory leve producers and firms would plan to reduce the production.

It will reduce the demand for factor servies and factor incomes. As a result the total volume of saving generated in the economy would fall or remain unchanged.

Question 5. Measure the level of ex-ante aggregate demand when autonomous investment and consumption expenditure (A) is ₹ 50 crores, and MPS is 0.2 and level of income (Y) is ₹ 4,000 crores. State whether the economy is in equilibrium or not (cite reasons).

Answer   Aggregate demand is given as

$$AD = \bar{A} + b\,(y)$$
$$\bar{A} = 50,\ MPC\,(b) = 1 - MPS$$
$$= 1 - 0.2 = 0.8$$

After putting values AD = 50 + 0.8 × 4,000

$$= ₹\ 3{,}250\ crores$$

Result   AD of ₹ 3,250 crores in less then Y (income) of ₹ 4,000 crores. Hence, the economy is not at equilibrium.

Question 6.   Explain 'paradox of thrift'.

Answer **Effective Demand** Effective demand refers to that level of aggregate demand which is 'effective' because it is equal to aggregate supply. We assume a constant price of final goods and constant rate of interest over short-run to determine the level of aggregate demand for final goods in the economy and also assume that the aggregate supply is perfectly elastic at this price.

5

Government Budget and the Economy

Points to Remember

1. **Government Budget** A government budget is an annual statement showing receipts and expenditures during a fiscal year.

2. **Objectives of Government Budget**
   (i) Economic growth
   (ii) Proper allocation of resources
   (iii) Generation of employment
   (iv) Economic stability
   (v) Economic equality
   (vi) Management of public enterprises

3. **Public Goods** Those goods which can not be provided through the market mechanism and hence, must be provided by the government are called public goods.

4. **Revenue Receipts** Receipt which neither create liability nor lead to reduction in assets are called revenue receipts. Revenue receipts are further divided under two heads
   (i) **Receipt from Tax**
       (a) Direct Tax
       (b) Indirect Tax
   (ii) **Receipts from Non-Tax Revenue**

5. **Capital Receipts** The receipts of government which create liability or reduce financial assets are called capital receipts.

   These receipts are classified under the following heads
   (i) Market borrowings
   (ii) Other borrowings and loans
   (iii) Small savings
   (iv) Provident fund and other deposits

6. **Revenue Expenditure** It refers to the expenditure that does not result in the creation of assets reduction of liabilities.

   The revenue expenditure is also of two types
   (i) Plan revenue expenditure
   (ii) Non-plan revenue expenditure

7. **Capital Expenditure** It refers to the expenditure which leads to creation of assets or reduction in liabilities. *e.g.*, defence capital, purchasing land, building etc.

8. **Plan Expenditure** The expenditure to be incurred during the financial year on the development and investment programmes under the current Five Year Plan is termed as plan expenditure.

9. **Non-Plan Expenditure** All expenditures of government not included in the current Five-Year Plan is termed as non-plan expenditure.

10. **Deficit Budget** If government expenditures exceed the government receipts, it is called deficit budget.
    (i) **Revenue Deficit** (RD) = Total Revenue Expenditure – Total Revenue Receipts
    (ii) **Fiscal Deficit** (FD) = Total Budget Expenditure – Total Budget Receipts excluding borrowing
    Or Fiscal Deficit = Borrowing
    (iii) **Primary Deficit** (PD)= Fiscal Deficit Interest Payment

11. **Measures to Reduce Fiscal Deficit**
    (i) Reduce public expenditure
    (ii) Increasing revenue from taxation and other measures

12. **Discretionary Fiscal Policy** If investment falls and government spending can be raised so that autonomous expenditure and equilibrium remain the same. This deliberate action to stabilise the economy is often referred to as discretionary fiscal policy.

QR Code Questions

Question 1. Which among the following is not a function of money?

    (a) It serves as a unit of account

    (b) It supports the barter system

    (c) It is a medium of exchange

    (d) It acts as a store of value

Answer   (b) It supports the barter system

    This concept is explained in Chapter-3 (Part-B) of NCERT Book.

Question 2. What will be the impact on government revenue when the cigarette prices are increased, assuming demand for cigarettes is inelastic?

    (a) Government revenue will increase

    (b) Government revenue will decrease

    (c) No effect on government revenue

    (d) None of the above

Answer   (a) Government revenue will increase

Question 3. Mention the correct year for each from the following
2016, 2015, 2017, 2014

    (i) Pradhan Mantri Awas Yojana ......

    (ii) Implementation of GST ......

    (iii) Make in India .....

    (iv) Demonetisation .....

Answer   (i) 2015   (ii) 2017   (iii) 2014   (iv) 2016

Question 4. Borrowing in government budget is

    (a) Fiscal Deficit   (b) Deficit in Taxes

    (c) Revenue Deficit   (d) Primary Deficit

Answer   (a) Fiscal Deficit

Question 5. The concept of Goods and Service Tax (GST) originated in

    (a) Korea   (b) Germany

    (c) Australia   (d) Canada

Answer   (d) Canada

Question 6.

Which of the following tax was abolished by the introduction of GST?

    (a) Corporation tax (b) Income Tax   (c) Sales Tax   (d) Wealth Tax

Answer (c) Sales Tax

Question 7. Fiscal deficit is the difference between the government's total expenditure and its total receipts, excluding borrowings. As per Union Budget 2018-19, what is the revised fiscal deficit target?

    (a) 3.2   (b) 3.3   (c) 3.7   (d) 3.6

Answer (b) 3.3

Question 8. Revenue deficit refers to the excess of government's revenue expenditure over revenue receipt. Revenue deficit is calculated after deducting .... from revenue expenditure.

    (a) revenue receipt   (b) revenue from disinvestment
    (c) non-tax revenue   (d) fiscal deficit

Answer (a) revenue receipt

Question 9.

Clean Environment Cess is imposed on

 (a) air pollution by factories
 (b) pollution of rivers
 (c) production of coal
 (d) cutting of trees

Answer (c) production of coal

Question 10. In which city the government proposes to set-up an institute to train manpower required for handling high-speed railway projects?

 (a) Surat   (b) Vadodara
 (c) Mumbai   (d) Jaipur

Answer (b) Vadodara

Question 11. As per the Union budget 2018, which scheme among the following will be launched to improve the health sector of the country?

 (a) Swath Bharat
 (b) National Health Policy, 2018
 (c) National Health Protection Scheme
 (d) Rashtriya Swasthya Bima Yojana

Answer (c) National Health Protection Scheme

Question 12. What is full form of GST?

 (a) Goods and Services Tax
 (b) Goods and Services Turnover
 (c) Gross Service Tax
 (d) Goods Service Tax

Answer (a) Goods and Services Tax

Question 13. What is full form of VAT?

 (a) Value Associate Tax
 (b) Value Added Turnover
 (c) Value Added Tax
 (d) Value Assets Tax

Answer (c) Value Added Tax

Question 14. What is full form of BHIM?

    (a) Bank Interface for Money

    (b) Bharat Interface for Money

    (c) Bharat Hindi Interface Money

    (d) Bharat Hindustan Interface for Money

Answer   (b) Bharat Interface for Money

Question 15. What is full form of NPA?

    (a) Non-performing Assets

    (b) Net Performing Assests

    (c) Non-perform Assests

    (d) National Performing Assests

Answer   (a) Non-performing Assets

Exercises

Question 1. Explain why public goods must be provided by the government?

Answer Public goods are refer to certain goods such as national defence, roads, government administration which cannot be provided through the market mechanism must be provided by the government.

These goods are necessary for life and national development. Presence and supply of these goods can not be ignored. An private sector enterprises do not take interest in it because these goods are not more profitable. So, government supplied the public goods.

Question 2. Distinguish between revenue expenditure and capital expenditure.

Answer

S.No	Revenue Expenditure	Capital Expenditure
1.	It neither creates any assets nor reduce any liability.	It either creates an asset or reduce a liability.
2.	It is incurred for normal running of governmental departments and various services.	It is incurred mainly for acquiring assets and granting loans.
3.	It is recurring in nature as day-to-day activities.	It is non-recurring in nature.
4.	Its examples-salary, pension, interest etc.	Its examples-repayment of loan, acquisition of asset etc.

Question 3. 'The fiscal deficit gives the borrowing requirement of the government'. Elucidate.

Answer   Fiscal deficit refers to excess of government expenditure over its receipts exclusive of borrowing. Thus, fiscal deficit points to borrowings requirement of the government to cope with its expenditure of the year. Higher borrowing implies higher burden of repayments of loans and of interest on the future generation.

As this burden mounts up, year after year, resource base future generation tends to shrink. This will definitely retard the process of future growth. Particularly, when borrowings by the government are used for non-productive purpose.

Question 4. Give the relationship between the revenue deficit and the fiscal deficit.

Answer   Revenue deficit is the excess of revenue expenditure of the government over its revenue receipts fiscal deficit is the excess of total budget expenditure over total budget receipts excluding borrowing. Fiscal deficit points to borrowing requirement of the government. As fiscal deficit mount up, increasingly larger part of GDP siphoned off to pay the existing loans.

Accordingly, resources available for revenue expenditure are reduced. Growth process is hindered. The government is once again compelled to take loans adding to its fiscal deficit.

Thus, revenue deficit and fiscal deficit tend to push up each other.

Question 5. Suppose that for a particular economy, investment is equal to 200, government purchases are 150, net taxes (that is lump-sum taxes minus transfers) is 100 and consumption is given by $C = 100 + 0.75\,y$

  (i) What is the level of equilibrium income?
  (ii) Calculate the value of the government expenditure multiplier and the tax multiplier.
  (iii) If the government expenditure increases by 200, find the change in equilibrium income.

Answer   Given, $I = 200$; $G = 150$; $T = 100$

$\quad\quad\quad C = 100 + 0.75\,Y$; $\overline{C} = 100$; $c = 0.75$

  (i) Equilibrium level of income
$$Y = \frac{1}{1-c}(\overline{C} - cT + I + G)$$

$$= \frac{1}{1-0.75}(100 - 0.75 \times 100 + 200 + 150)$$

$$= \frac{1}{0.25}(375) = \frac{375}{25} \times 100 = ₹\,1,500$$

(ii) Government expenditure multiplier

$$\frac{\Delta Y}{\Delta G} = \frac{1}{1-c} = \frac{1}{1-0.75} = \frac{1}{0.25}$$

$$\frac{1}{25} \times 100 = 4$$

$$\text{Tax multiplier} = \frac{\Delta Y}{\Delta T} = \frac{-c}{1-c} = \frac{-0.75}{1-0.75} = \frac{-0.75}{0.25} = \frac{-75}{25} = -3$$

(iii) New equilibrium income

$$\frac{1}{1-c}[\bar{C} - cT + I + G + \Delta G]$$

$$= \frac{1}{1-0.75}[100 - 0.75 \times 100 + 200 + 150 + 200]$$

$$= \frac{1}{0.25} \times 575$$

$$= \frac{575}{25} \times 100 = 2,300$$

Change in equilibrium income = 2,300 − 1,500 = 800

Question 6. Consider an economy described by the following function : $C = 20 + 0.80y, I = 30, G = 50, \text{TR} = 100$

(i) Find the equilibrium level of income and the autonomous expenditure multiplier in the model.

(ii) If government expenditure increases by 30, what is the impact on equilibrium income?

(iii) If a lump sum tax of 30 is added to pay for the increase in government purchases, how will equilibrium income change?

Answer $I = 30;\ \Delta G = 30;\ G = 50;\ T = 100;\ c = 0.80$

$$C = 20 + 0.80 = Y$$

(i) Equilibrium level of income

$$Y = \frac{1}{1-c}[\bar{C} - cT + I + G] = \frac{1}{1-0.80}[20 + 0.80 \times 100 + 30 + 50]$$

$$= \frac{1}{0.20}[180] = \frac{180}{20} \times 100 = 900$$

Expenditure multiplier

$$\frac{1}{1-c} = \frac{1}{1-0.80} = \frac{1}{0.20} = \frac{100}{20} = 5$$

(ii) Increase in government expenditure

$$= \frac{1}{1-c}[\overline{C} + cT + I + G + \Delta G]$$

$$= \frac{1}{1-0.80}[20 + 0.80 \times 100 + 30 + 50 + 30]$$

$$= \frac{1}{0.20}[210] = \frac{210}{20} \times 100 = 1,050$$

(iii) Tax multiplier $= \dfrac{-c}{1-c}$

$$\frac{\Delta Y}{\Delta T} = \frac{-c}{1-c}$$

$$\Delta Y = \frac{-c}{1-c} \times \Delta T = \frac{-0.80}{1-0.80} \times 30 = \frac{-80}{20} \times 30 = -120$$

New equilibrium level of income $= Y + \Delta Y = 900 + (-120) = 780$

Question 7. In the above question, calculate the effect on output of a 10% increase in transfers, and a 10% increase in lump sum taxes. Compare the effect of two.

Answer   MPC $= 0.80$; $\overline{C} = 20$; $I = 30$; $G = 50$

$$TR = 100; \ \Delta TR = 10$$

Equilibrium level of income

$$= \frac{1}{1-c}[\overline{C} + cTR + I + G + \Delta TR]$$

$$= \frac{1}{1-0.80}[20 + 0.80 \times 100 + 30 + 50 + 0.80 \times 10]$$

$$= \frac{188}{20} \times 100 = 940$$

Change in income $= 940 - 900 = 40$

Increase in lump sum tax $\Delta T = 10$

$$\text{Change in income} = \Delta T \times \frac{-c}{1-c}$$

$$= -10 \times \frac{0.80}{0.20} = -10 \times 4 = -40$$

Conclusion   Increase of 10% in transfers will raise the income by 40 and increase of 10% in tax will lead to fall in the income by 40.

Quesstion 8. We suppose that

$$C = 70 + 0.70Y \ D, I = 90, G = 100, T = 0.10y$$

(i) Find the equilibrium income.

(ii) What are tax revenues at equilibrium income? Does the government have a balanced budget?

Answer

(i) $C = 70 + 0.70\,YD$; $I = 90$; $G = 100$; $T = 0.10\ Y$

$$Y = C + I + G = 70 + 0.70\,Y + 90 + 100$$
$$= 70 + 0.70\,YD + 190 = 70 + 0.70(Y - T) + 190$$
$$= 70 + 0.70\,Y - 0.70 \times 0.10\,Y + 190$$
$$= 70 + 0.70\,Y - 0.07Y + 190$$
$$= 70 + 0.63Y + 190 = 260 + 0.63Y$$

$$Y - 0.634 = 260$$
$$0.37Y = 260$$
$$Y = \frac{260}{0.37} = 702.7$$

(ii) $T = 0.10Y = 0.10 \times 702.7 = 70.27$

Government expenditure $= 100$

Tax revenue $= 70.27$

Government has a deficit budget, not a balanced budget because government expenditure exceeds the tax revenue. ($G > T$)

Question 9. Suppose marginal propensity to consume is 0.75 and there is a 20% proportional income tax. Find the change in equilibrium income for the following

   (i) Government purchases increase by 20

   (ii) Transfers decrease by 20

Answer

(i) $\Delta Y = \dfrac{1}{1 - c\,(1-t)} \times \Delta G = \dfrac{1}{1 - 0.75\,(1 - 0.2)} \times 20$

$$= \dfrac{1}{1 - 0.75 \times 0.8} \times 20$$

$$= \dfrac{20}{1 - 0.60} = \dfrac{20}{0.4} = 50$$

(ii) $\Delta Y = \dfrac{c}{1 - c}\,\Delta T = \dfrac{0.75}{1 - 0.75} \times 20 = \dfrac{0.75}{0.25} \times 20 = 60$

Question 10. Explain why the tax multiplier is smaller in absolute value than the government expenditure multiplier?

Answer   The tax multiplier is negative, implies an increase in taxes leads to fall in output it is smaller in absolute value than the spending multiplier we can say higher taxes reduces the people's disposable income, thereby reducing their consumption.

Explaination by taxing an example

Suppose MPC = 0.90

Government expenditure multiplier $= \dfrac{1}{1-0.90} = \dfrac{1}{0.10} = \dfrac{100}{10} = 10$

Tax multiplier $= \dfrac{-c}{1-c} = \dfrac{-0.90}{1-0.90} = \dfrac{-0.90}{0.10} = -9$

Thus, it is clear that government expenditure multiplier is more than the tax multiplier.

Question 11. Explain the relation between government deficit and government debt.

Answer The concepts of deficit and debt are closely related. Deficit can be thought of as a flow which add to the stock of debt. If the government continues to borrow year after year, it leads to the accumulation of debt and the government has to pay more and more by way of interest.These interest payments themselves contribute to the debt.

Question 12. Does public debt impose a burden? Explain.

Answer Yes, public debt impose a burden in the following cases
   (i) When government has imposed new taxes or raised the existing tax rates to repay the debt.
   (ii) When public debt is taken for war purposes or debt is used in an unplanned manner.
   (iii) When debt is to be redeemed by issuing of new currency it will cause inflation in the country.

Question 13. Are fiscal deficit inflationary?

Answer Yes, if fiscal deficit is financed by issuing new currency it will increase inflation. It may be worsen if new currency used to finance the current consumption expenditure of the government. It new money is used for infrastructural activities or other capital projects, then fiscal deficit will not to be inflationary.

Question 14. Discuss the issue of deficit reduction.

Answer The deficit can be reduced through the following
   (i) **Increase in Receipts** Government can impose new taxes or increase rate of existing taxes to increase its receipts. Receipts reduce the deficit.
   (ii) **Decrease in Expenditure** Government can reduce the deficit by reduce its unproductive and administrative expenditure and also encourages to private sector to undertake capital projects to reduce its expenditure.

Question 15. What do you understand by GST? How good is the system of GST as compared to the old tax system? State its categories.

Answer Goods and Services Tax (GST) is the single comprehensive indirect tax, operational from 1st July, 2017, on supply of goods and services, right from the manufacturer/service provider to the consumer.

It is a destination based consumption tax with facility of Input Tax Credit in the supply chain. It is applicable throughout the country with one rate for one type of good/service. It has replaced large number of taxes on goods and services levied on production/sale of goods or provision of services, such as Central Excise Duty, Service Tax, Central Sales Tax, VAT/Sales Tax, etc. In the old tax regime, taxes were imposed on the value added at each stage, as well as, on the total value. This escalated the price.

The GST regime is superior in the following aspects

   (i) GST has simplified the multiplicity of taxes on goods and services.

   (ii) The laws and rates of taxes across the country are standardised.

   (iii) It has facilitated the freedom of movement of goods and services and created a common market in the country.

   (iv) It is aimed at reducing the cost of business operations and cascading effect of various taxes on consumers. It has also reduced the overall cost of production which will make Indian products/ services more competitive in the domestic and international markets.

   (v) It will also result into higher economic growth.

   (vi) Compliance will also be easier as all tax payment related services like registration, returns, payments are available online through a common portal www.gst.gov.in.

   (vii) It has expanded the tax base, introduced higher transparency in the taxation system, reduced human interface between taxpayer and government and is furthering ease of doing business.

The following are its categories

   (i) Central GST (CGST)

   (ii) State GST (SGST)

   (iii) Union Territory GST (UTGST)

6

Open Economy Macroeconomics

Points to Remember

1. **Open Economy** It is one in which trading is done with other nations in goods and service and most often in financial assets.

2. **Balance of Payment** It is a systematic record of all economic transaction between the residents of a country and the rest of the world during a year.

3. **Current Account** Transactions relating to trade in goods and services and transfer payment constitute the current account.

   Components of Current Account

   (i) Visible Trade (ii) Invisible Trade (iii) Transfer Payment

4. **Capital Account** It represents international capital transactions which include sale and purchase of assets such as bonds equities, lands , loans, bank account etc.

   Components of capital account

   (i) Foreign Investment
   (ii) Loans
   (iii) Banking Capital Transaction

5. **Balance of Trade** It means the systematic records of visible imports and exports in a given year.

$$BoT = \text{Visible Exports} - \text{Visible Imports}$$

6. **Autonomous Transaction** It refers to those international economic transaction which are taken with the motive of profit.

7. **Accommodating Items** All the items related to the monetary transfers correcting balance of payments disequilibrium are accommodating items.

8. **Foreign Exchange Market** The market in which foreign currencies are bought and sold is called the foreign exchange market.

9. **Foreign Exchange Rate** The rate at which one currency is exchanged for other is known as the rate of exchanges or foreign exchange rate.

10. **Fixed Exchange Rate System** It refers to the rate of exchange fixed by the government.

    It has two important variants

    (i) Gold standard system of exchange rate.

    (ii) Bretton woods system of exchange rate.

11. **Determination of Foreign Exchange Rate** It is determined by the forces of supply and demand in the foreign exchange market.

12. **Devaluation** It is the fall in the value of domestic currency in relation to foreign currency as planned by the government. In a situation exchange rate is fixed by government.

13. **Depreciation** It is the fall in the value of domestic currency in relation to foreign currency in a situation when exchange rate is determined by the forces of demand and supply in the international money market.

14. **Managed Floating** It is a system that allows adjustments in exchanges rate according to set of rules and regulation which are officially declared in the foreign exchanges market.

QR Code Questions

Question 1. Choose the correct headquarters of each from the following

New York, Geneva, Paris, Washington DC

(i) IMF　　(ii) OECD　　(iii) WTO　　(iv) United Nation

Answer　(i) Washington DC　(ii) Paris　(iii) Geneva　(iv) New York

Question 2. The price of one currency in terms of the other is known as the ....

(a) Reserve Repo Rate　　　　(b) Repo Rate

(c) Exchange Rate　　　　(d) Purchasing Power Parity

Answer　(c) Exchange Rate

Question 3. When import is more than export, then .... occurs.
    (a) excess supply   (b) trade surplus
    (c) excess demand   (d) trade deficit

Answer   (d) trade deficit

Question 4.

Countries often impose restrictions on free foreign trade
    (a) to protect domestic producer
    (b) to protect foreign producer
    (c) to protect foreign consumer
    (d) to protect domestic consumers

Answer   (a) to protect domestic producer

Question 5.

In international trade if the domestic price of goods is more than the world price

(a) the country will neither import nor export
(b) the country will become an importer of the goods
(c) additional information is required
(d) the country will become an exporter of the goods

Answer (b) the country will become an importer of the goods

Question 6. Identify the logo

(a) World Bank
(b) International Monetary Fund
(c) United Nation
(d) World Health Organisation

Answer (d) World Health Organisation

Question 7. Identify the logo

(a) United Nation
(b) World Bank
(c) International Monetary Fund
(d) World Trade Organisation

Answer (a) United Nation

Question 8. Identify the logo

   (a) United Nation   (b) World Health Organisation
   (c) World Trade Organisation   (d) World Bank

Answer   (c) World Trade Organisation

Question 9. Identify the logo

   (a) International Monetary Fund
   (b) World Trade Organisation
   (c) International Labour Organisation
   (d) World Bank

Answer   (d) World Bank

Question 10. Identify the currency

   (a) Pound   (b) Euro
   (c) Dollar   (d) Yen

Answer   (c) Dollar

Question 11. Identify the currency

   (a) Rupee   (b) Yen   (c) Pound   (d) Dollar

Answer (b) Yen

Question 12. Identify the currency

   (a) Euro   (b) Dollar   (c) Pound   (d) Yen

Answer (a) Euro

Question 13. Identify the currency

   (a) Dollar   (b) Pound   (c) Yen   (d) Euro

Answer (b) Pound

Question 14. Which of the following excludes interest payments?
   (a) Revenue deficit   (b) Fiscal deficit
   (c) Primary deficit

Answer (c) Primary deficit

Question 15. If India has a trade deficit with the US, to eliminate this gap rupee should .... against the dollar.
   (a) weaken   (b) compete   (c) strengthen

Answer (a) weaken

Exercises

Question 1. Differentiate between balance of trade and current account balance.

Answer Difference between balance of trade and current account balance

	Balance of Trade	Current Account Balance
1.	It is a difference between exports and imports of goods.	It is net value of balances of visible and of invisible trade of unilaterel transfer.
2.	Balance of Trade includes only visible items.	Current account records both visible and invisible items.
3.	It is a narrow concepts means it is only a part of current account balance.	It is a wider concept and it includes balance of trades.

Question 2. What are official reserve transactions? Explain their importance in the balance of payments.

Answer Official reserve refers to that the monetary authority (central bank) is financed the any deficit in the balance of payment.

Official reserve transactions take place when a country withdraws from its stock of foreign exchange reserves to finance deficit in its overall balance of payment. A country with surplus in its overall BoP leads to rise in foreign exchanges reserves.

Importance Official reserve transactions help to bring a balance in the country's overall balance of payment. So, it plays an important role in economy of any country.

Question 3. Distinguish between the nominal exchange rate and the real exchange rate. If you were to decide whether to buy domestic goods or foreign goods, which rate would be more relevant? Explain.

Answer **Nominal Exchange Rate**   It means the price of foreign currency in terms of domestic currency. Means, the number of units of domestic currency one must give up to get an unit of foreign currency.

Real Exchange Rate   It refers to the relative price of foreign goods in terms of domestic goods.

To buy domestic goods of foreign goods, at a point of time nominal exchange rate is more relevant.

Question 4. Suppose it takes 1.25 yen to buy a rupee, and the price level in Japan is 3 and the price level in India is 1.2. Calculate the real exchange rate between India and Japan.

Answer   Given $= P =$ Price Level in India $= 1.2$

$$P_f = \text{Price Level in Japan} = 3$$

$$e = \text{Nominal Exchanges Rate} = \frac{1}{1.25} = 0.8$$

$\therefore$ Real Exchange Rate $= \dfrac{eP_f}{P}$

$$= \frac{0.8 \times 3}{1.2} = 2$$

Question 5. Explain the automatic mechanism by which BoP equilibrium was achieved under the gold standard.

Answer   The country from which we were importing and marking payment in gold would face an increase in prices and cost. There would be disequilibrium.

Normally the BoP of the country losing gold and worsen that of the country with the favourable trade balance, until equilibrium in international trade is re-established at relative prices that keep import and export in balance with no further net gold flow. Thus, fixed exchange rates were maintained by an automatic equilibrating mechanism.

Question 6. How is the exchange rate determined under the flexible exchange rate regime?

Answer   Flexible exchange rate is determined by the forces of supply and demand in the international market. And the equilibrium exchange rate is determined at a level where demand for foreign exchange is equal to the supply of foreign exchange.

- Sources of demand for foreign exchange
    - (i) Payment of international loans
    - (ii) Gifts and grants to rest of the world
- Source of supply of foreign exchange
    - (i) Export to the rest of the world
    - (ii) Direct foreign investment
    - (iii) Direct purchase of goods and services by the non-residents in the domestic market.

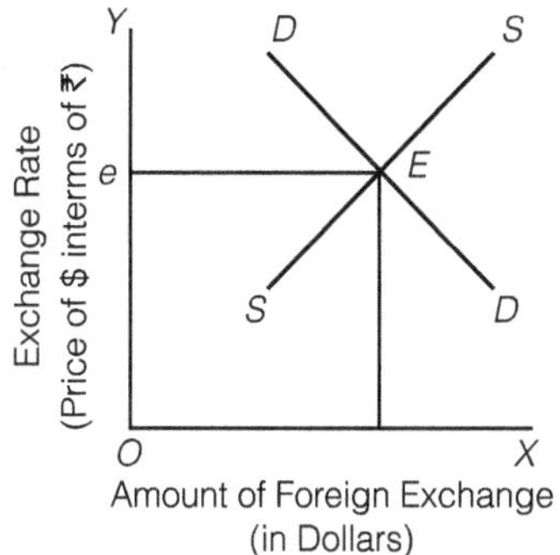

In the figure, the equilibrium exchange rate *i.e., E*

Question 7. Differentiate between devaluation and depreciation

Answer   Difference between devaluation and depreciation

	Devaluation	Depreciation
1.	It means the decrease in the price of domestic currency under fixed exchange rates.	It means decrease in the price of the domestic currency in terms of the floating exchange rates.
2.	It takes place due to official action (by government).	It takes place due to market forces.
3.	It takes place under fixed (pegged) exchange rate system.	It takes place under flexible exchange rate system.

Question 8. Would the central bank need to intervene in a managed floating system? Explain why.

Answer   Managed floating is a system that allows adjustment in exchange rate according to set of rules and regulations which are officially declared in the foreign market. Under this system, also called dirty floating, central banks intervene to buy and sell foreign currency in an attempt to moderate exchange rate movements whenever they feel that such action are appropriate. Official reserve transaction are therefore, not equal to zero.

Question 9. Are the concepts of demand for domestic goods and domestic demand for goods the same?

Answer   No, both concept are not same demand for domestic goods refers the demand for goods made by both domestic and foreign countries. Domestic demand for goods refers the demand for goods by our own country for goods which may be produced in foreign countries.

Question 10. What is the marginal propensity to import when $M = 60 + 0.6Y$? What is the relationship between the marginal propensity to import and the aggregate demand function?

Answer Marginal propensity to import indicates the extent to which imports are induced by changes in income of production.

It is given
$$M = 60 + 0.06Y$$
$$M = M + MY$$

$\therefore$ Here (m) Marginal propensity to import $= 0.06$

The marginal propensity to import negatively affects the aggregate demand function.

When income increase aggregate demand decreases. This is because the additional income is spent on foreign goods and not on domestic goods.

Question 11. Why is the open economy autonomous expenditure multiplier smaller than the closed economy one?

Answer The open economy multiplier is smaller than in a closed economy because a part of domestic demand falls on foreign goods. An increase in autonomous demand leads to a smaller increase in output compared to a closed economy.

Question 12. Calculate the open economy multiplier with proportional taxes, $T = tY$, instead of lump-sum taxes as assumed in the text.

Answer $y = C + c(1-t)Y + I + G + X - M - my$

$$Y - c(1-t)Y + my = C + I + G + X - M$$
$$Y[1 - c(1-t) + m] = C + I + G + X - M$$
$$Y = \frac{C + I + G + X - M}{[1 - c(1-t) + m]}$$

Autonomous Expenditure $(A) = C + I + G - m + X - m$

$\therefore$ Open economy multiplie with proportional taxes

$$\frac{\Delta Y}{\Delta A} = \frac{1}{1 - c(1-t) + m}$$

Question 13. Suppose $C = 40 + 0.8YD, T = 50, I = 60, G = 40, X = 90$.
$$M = 50 + 0.05Y$$

(i) Find equilibrium income.

(ii) Find the net export balance at equilibrium income.

(iii) What happens to equilibrium income and the net export balance when the government purchases increase fron 40 to 50?

Answer   Given, $C = 40 + 0.8\,YD$, $T = 50$, $I = 60$, $G = 40$, $X = 90$

$$M = 50 + 0.05Y$$

(i) Equilibrium level of income

$$Y = C + c\,(Y - T) + I + G + X - M - mY$$

$$Y = \frac{A}{1 - c + m}, \qquad \text{Here } A = C - CT + I + G + X - M$$

$$= \frac{C - cT + I + G + X + M}{1 - c + m}$$

$$= \frac{40 - 0.8 \times 50 + 60 + 40 + 90 - 50}{1 - 0.8 + 0.05}$$

$$= \frac{140}{0.25} = \frac{140}{25} \times 100 = 560$$

(ii) Net export at equilibrium income

$$NX = X - M - mY$$

$$= 90 - 50 - 0.05 \times 560 = 40 - 28 = 12$$

(iii) If G increases from 40 to 50

$$Y = \frac{C - cT + I + G + X - M}{1 - c + m}$$

$$= \frac{40 - 0.8 \times 50 + 60 + 50 + 90 - 50}{1 - 0.8 + 0.05}$$

$$= \frac{40 - 40 + 60 + 50 + 40}{0.25} = \frac{150}{0.25} = \frac{150}{25} \times 100 = 600$$

Net export balance

$$NX = X - M - mY$$

$$= 90 - 50 - 0.05 \times 600 = 40 - 30 = 10$$

Question 14. In the above example, if exports change to $X = 100$, find the change in equilibrium income and the net export balance.

Answer Given, $C = 40 + 0.8\,YD$, $T = 50$, $I = 60$, $G = 40$, $X = 100$

$$M = 50 + 0.0\,5Y$$

$$\text{Equilibrium income } = \frac{C - cT + I + G + X - M}{1 - c + m}$$

$$= \frac{40 - 0.8 \times 50 + 40 + 60 + 100 - 50}{1 - 0.8 + 0.05}$$

$$= \frac{40 - 40 + 100 + 100 - 50}{0.25}$$

$$= \frac{150}{25} \times 100 = 600$$

$$Nx = X - M - my$$

Net export balance

$$Nx = X - M - 0.05\,Y$$
$$= 100 - 50 - 0.05 \times 600 = 50 - 30 = 20$$

Question 15. Suppose the exchange rate between the rupee and the dollar was ₹ 30=1$ in the year 2010. Suppose the prices have doubled in India over 20 years while they have remained fixed in USA. What according to the purchasing power parity theory will be the exchange rate between dollar and rupee in the year 2030?

Answer The rupee-dollar exchange rate = ₹ 30 = $ 1. So, if we want to buy a bar of chocolate, then it would cost ₹ 30 in India and $ 1 in America. By 2030, the price have doubled in India. So, now a bar of chocolate would cost ₹ 60 in India and $ 1 in America. So, now the rupee-dollar exchange rate will be ₹ 60 = $ 1.

Question 16. If inflation is higher in country A than in country B, and the exchange rate between the two countries is fixed, what is likely to happen to the trade balance between the two countries?

Answer The exchange rate is one of the most important determinant of a country. It plays a vital role in the country's level of trade. As per the above condition it is favourable for country A to import goods and on the other hand for country B export is favourable.

There would be no balance in trade between the two countries as country A is importing more goods as compared to exports which results in trade deficit and on the other hand country B suffers from trade surplus because they are focusing more on exports than imports.

Question 17. Should a current account deficit be a cause for alarm? Explain.

Answer A current account deficit means that the value of imports for goods and services are greater than the value of exports it leads to several causes which are

   (i) Due to fixed exchange rate exports will become uncompetitive.

   (ii) Economic growth is not favourable.

   (iii) Inflation and borrowings become the major problems.

Thus, we can say that current account deficit be a cause for alarm because the value of exports increased at a slow rate than the imports and there is an increase in the deficit or we can say surplus changed into deficit.

Question 18. Suppose $C = 100 + 0.75YD$, $I = 500$, $G = 750$, taxes are 20% of income, $X = 150$, $M = 100 + 0.2Y$.

Calculate equilibrium income, the budget deficit or surplus and the trade deficit or surplus.

Answer $C = 100 + 0.75\, YD$, $I = 500$, $G = 750$, $X = 150$

$$M = 100 + 0.2\, Y$$

Equilibrium income $= C + c\,(Y - T) + I + G + X - M - mY$

$$Y = 100 + .75\left(Y - \frac{20}{100}Y\right) + 500 + 750 + 150 - 100 - 0.2Y$$

$$Y = 1{,}400 + \frac{75}{100} \times \frac{44}{5} - 0.2Y$$

$$= 1{,}400 + \frac{3}{5}Y - o.2Y$$

$$Y = \frac{64}{10} = 1{,}400 = 750$$

$$\text{Government tax} = \frac{20}{100} \times \frac{7{,}000}{3} = \frac{1{,}400}{3} = 466.6$$

Government expenditure > Government receipts

It shows budget deficit

$$NX = X - M - mY = 150 - 100 - \frac{2}{10} \times \frac{7{,}000}{3}$$

$$= 150 - 100 - 466.66$$

$$= -416.66$$

Here, NX is negative.

Thus, it implies trade deficit.

Question 19. Discuss some of the exchange rate arrangements that countries have entered into to bring about stability in their external accounts.

Answer Exchange rate expresses the ratio of exchange between the currencies of two countries.'

Mostly three exchange rate used to bring about stability in their external accounts by countries.

1. **Fixed Exchanged Rate** The exchange rate that is official fixed and declared by the government.

There are two kinds of fixed exchange rate

(i) **Gold Standard System**   As per this system gold was taken as the common unit of parity between currencies of different countries in the circulation. Each country was to define value of its currency in terms of the other currency was fixed considering gold value of each currency.

(ii) **The Bretton Woods System** As per this system all currencies were pegged or related to US dollar at a fixed exchange rate. This system gave birth to international and monetary fund as the central institution in the international monetary system.

2. **Flexible Exchange Rate**   The exchange rate which is determined by the forces of demand and supply of different and currencies in the foreign exchange market.

   It is a flexible rate because the value of currency is allowed to fluctuate according to change in demand and supply of foreign exchange.

3. **Managed Floating Rate System** The system in which the central bank allows the exchange rate to be determined by market forces but intervence at times to influence the rate. For this, central bank maintains reserves of foreign exchange to ensure that the exchange rate stays with in the targated value.